THE GURUBOOK

THE GURUBOOK

THE GURUBOOK

INSIGHTS FROM 45 PIONEERING ENTREPRENEURS AND LEADERS ON BUSINESS STRATEGY AND INNOVATION

By Jonathan Løw

Routledge
Taylor & Francis Group

A PRODUCTIVITY PRESS BOOK

CRC Press
Taylor & Francis Group
6000 Broken Sound Parkway NW, Suite 300
Boca Raton, FL 33487-2742

© 2018 by Jonathan Løw
CRC Press is an imprint of Taylor & Francis Group, an Informa business

No claim to original U.S. Government works

Printed on acid-free paper

International Standard Book Number-13: 978-1-138-56656-9 (Hardback)
International Standard Book Number-13: 978-1-138-56643-9 (Paperback)
International Standard Book Number-13: 978-1-315-12375-2 (eBook)

Visit the Taylor & Francis Web site at
http://www.taylorandfrancis.com

and the CRC Press Web site at
http://www.crcpress.com

THE WORLD IS GIVING YOU
ANSWERS EVERY DAY.
LEARN TO LISTEN.

CONTENTS

CONTENTS

JONATHAN LØW
Introduction

GuruBook editor Jonathan Løw is a Danish entrepreneur and co-founder of four startups. He has been named one of Denmark's 100 most talented leaders and has won a number of startup awards. In addition to being an entrepreneur, Jonathan Løw is the former Head of Marketing at the KaosPilots, investor at Accelerace, and Head of Online at Bog & idé. His previous book, *Listen Louder*, made it to the top of the bestseller lists in 2015. For more information, speaking engagements, and so on, please check out www.listenlouder.dk.

gu·ru (gur' ü, gü' rü, also gə rü'), *n.*
: a teacher or mentor whom you trust.
: a person who has great experience or knowledge within a particular area.

Ideas

As human beings, we have always been fascinated by ideas. The ancient Greek philosophers Plato and Aristotle spoke about ideas as something that structured the world and made it understandable for human consciousness. After the Greeks came the Latin Father Augustine, among others; he raised ideas to be a form of thinking in the mind of God.

Inspired by English empiricists such as Locke, Berkeley, and Hume, today we regard ideas as part of the human cognition. Ideas are something we humans get all the time—no matter whether we're at the office, in the bath, at a football match, or washing up. As ideas are an integral part of being human, generating ideas is something we all have in common. In fact, our brains can't do otherwise.

Ideas can be magical in the sense that we can dream of great and epic changes in the world if only our apparently brilliant idea can be turned into reality. In this way, an idea embodies something beautiful and childish.

On the other hand, one of the points in *The GuruBook* is that we cultivate thinking about good ideas far too much, while we cultivate the craft of transforming the ideas into reality far too little.

In future, the world will not exist on the basis of good ideas but on the talented craftsmen—entrepreneurs, innovators, and leaders—who, together with their competent teams, have the ability to move ideas out of the thought process and into reality.

Ideas are thus valueless in the sense that they do not make a difference by themselves. But their visionary and potentially transformative character can still function today as a fantastic incentive and motivator—such as when the authors of the international bestseller *BOLD* introduced the idea that tomorrow's billionaires are those whose inventions and businesses also help a billion people.

The change-making ideas of the present are thus those which, although based on great thinking, require less action to turn those ideas into reality. Today, it is the experiments, the prototypes, and the actions that help us test the durability and effects of an idea, and subsequently, the cleverest entrepreneurs, businesses, and public institutions that, through their commitment and resources, can make ideas change the world in practice. *That* is innovation and enterprise.

The GuruBook is in itself one example of such an entrepreneurial process. The book started with a stream of thought during an evening meal back in November 2015. I can remember thinking something like, "Imagine if one could gather all the thoughts from the world's most inspirational leaders, entrepreneurs, and innovators in one book in order to share them. Imagine if this could inspire others to be even better at turning the best ideas into reality."

The GuruBook is the materialization of that idea.

But perhaps it isn't really. For as the work progressed and I had to choose contributors, and the articles/interviews were received in due course from all corners of the world—from Shanghai to Silicon Valley—I realized that I wasn't aiming at pointing out the cleverest or the most prestigious entrepreneurs and leaders.

The GuruBook is not a hit list or an ultimate statement about who is "world leader" in their field. Rather, it's almost turned into a sort of "turning myself inside out" project—a desire to present the reader with the voices that I've found to be the most exciting, inspiring, and challenging to listen to in recent years.

Ability to listen

The GuruBook is first and foremost about listening. Although I have been a serial entrepreneur and have tried

to start a number of businesses, have worked with innovation in both large and small organizations, and have been a leader in several organizations, I do not imagine in any way that I have all the answers in these exciting but also complex areas.

I believe that the ability to listen is one of the most important characteristics for future entrepreneurs, innovators, and leaders. This ability to listen, and the curiosity that is inherent in it, may be the factor that gives you an advantage over the competition. Consider, for example, the English mathematician and physicist Isaac Newton, who, like millions of others, saw an apple fall from a tree. The difference was that Newton asked *why*.

As a result of my own curiosity and desire to listen more, it was obvious that I should invite the people who, in my eyes, have generated inspiring and pioneering ideas, organizations, and results, to share their thoughts and knowledge with the readers of *The GuruBook*.

This book's gurus have been asked to talk/write about what they're enthusiastic about. That means that you, dear reader, can look forward to becoming more knowledgeable about

- How to start a business without an idea
- Why some ideas succeed while others fail
- How to demystify the task of scaling up a startup as an entrepreneur
- How you can be enterprising, no matter what phase your organization is in
- How to create an innovative culture
- Why simple questions lead to the greatest innovations
- What we can learn from the world's leading innovators

- Why businesses and local authorities aren't start-ups, and what both can learn from each other
- How to become authentic as a leader
- Why authentic leadership is a strength
- Why there's an entrepreneur in every successful leader
- Why the ability to listen is all-important, whether you're an entrepreneur or a leader

The contents of *The GuruBook* have weight and value because the articles and/or interviews are with people who for years have perfected their ability to listen and have consistently become better at understanding their customers, partners, and colleagues. Through thousands of meetings, sales calls, customer service responses, innovation processes, brainstorms, mail dialogues, LinkedIn discussions, and so on, they have listened and then acted on what they heard. These are the insights that *The GuruBook* contains.

I fundamentally believe the future belongs to the curious. The future belongs to the entrepreneurs, innovators, leaders, and passionate souls who are not only capable of "listening more intently" to the world about them but who also have the ability to act on the input they get.

Authenticity and gurus

The GuruBook is made up of three pillars or major themes, if you like: *entrepreneurship*, *innovation*, and *authentic leadership*. Each of these three themes could be unfolded in numerous guru books on their own. As editor, therefore, I harbor no illusions that this book can touch on all aspects of three so broad and important concepts.

In the same way, the work in choosing the book's gurus has rather resembled the task facing a national football coach: to put together a team based on personal convictions, values, and attitudes without knowing for sure that the choices are the correct ones—just as I have been aware from the outset that the readers will have many strong and clear opinions about the team of gurus chosen.

There have also been many comments about the title of the book, so let me explain it with two short points:

I chose the title because I mean it!

It's not just in Hinduism that the word *guru* has a religious and solemn meaning. In itself, the word means "teacher" or "mentor." And that is precisely what the contributors to *The GuruBook* represent: wisdom and experience that is worth sharing with you, dear reader.

I chose the title because it sounds good!

Can't we agree that *The Expert Book* sounds neither as catchy nor as sexy as *The GuruBook*? So you shouldn't take the title more seriously than that.

Finally, discussions about gender politics and other demographics may soon arise when one tries to make up a guru team: Is the gender distribution fair? What about the age variation? The geographic spread? The ideological starting point?

I must put my cards on the table and say that I haven't thought along these lines. My most important criterion has been that I consider all the gurus in the book to be authentic, and authentic leadership therefore became the third main theme and pillar in *The GuruBook*.

Authentic in the way that they also act out their values in practice. Authentic in the sense that you can feel the person inside them when you speak with them. Authentic in the way that they dare to stand for something and remain true to their values—even when they come under financial or other pressure.

Action

I hope that *The GuruBook* is a book you'll listen to but also a book that you'll use as a background for your actions.

I haven't conceived the book as something to be read slavishly from start to finish in quest of a single truth or solution. On the other hand, I'll be happy if you leaf back and forth through the many contributions and if some texts make you put the book down and start something because you feel inspired. It is conceived to reach you where you are now. You may find some of the contributions banal, but these same texts could be a revelation to another reader. I hope—and I believe—that you'll perhaps get a clearer view of a problem that you're dealing with in your everyday work as an entrepreneur, as a leader, and not least as a human being.

That's the difference between knowledge and learning. *The GuruBook* gives you knowledge and visions in the form of its contributions. The subsequent learning—how this knowledge is converted into practice (the craft)—is something you're responsible for.

I would love to hear from you about how you've chosen to use the gurus' guidance and experience and my tools in your concrete everyday reality. If you wish, you are more than welcome to share your experiences with me. You can write to me at jonathan@listenlouder.dk or connect via LinkedIn.

Enjoy the book…
Jonathan Løw
—editor and creator of *The GuruBook*

ENTREPRENEURSHIP

INTRODUCTION

In the first theme of *The GuruBook—entrepreneurship—* the book's gurus give you input to a number of subjects, including

- How you start a business without an idea
- Why some ideas succeed while others fail
- What entrepreneurs can learn from established businesses and vice versa
- How you can be enterprising, no matter what phase your organization is in

As the book's editor and a serial entrepreneur, I know entrepreneurship as something that is inspirational, rewarding, demanding, and difficult. It is a craft where you are constantly developing and testing, getting inspiration, developing further, and starting over.

The majority of the successful entrepreneurs that I've met and talked with have at least one thing in common: they work on the basis of the following mantra.

Think big.
Act small.
Fail quickly and cheaply.

This means that they are driven by something that's larger than they are, and they have a desire to do something in the world that's smarter, better, more meaningful, more important. But as a rule, you start with limited resources and limited time, so you must act small and fail cheaply in order to be able to continue your journey toward the great goal.

Enjoy yourself in reaching your great goals in life; I hope this book can help you some of the way!

BLAKE MYCOSKIE
Giving is our future

Blake Mycoskie (United States) is a visionary leader and social entrepreneur. He is the founder and Chief Shoe Giver of TOMS and the brand's One for One® movement. Blake and TOMS have received various forms of recognition, including the Cannes Lion Heart Award.

The GuruBook is about visionary leaders and entrepreneurs. To me, Blake Mycoskie has always been one of those. Being the founder of TOMS and developing the brand's One for One movement, Mycoskie has been a frontrunner in the field of social entrepreneurship.

Today, TOMS is not only giving shoes to children in need for every pair purchased but has expanded to providing eyesight, safe water, safe births, antibullying initiatives, and solar light through the sales of eyewear, coffee, bags, and Apple Watch bands.

Blake and TOMS have received various forms of recognition, including the Cannes Lion Heart Award, which honors a person or company that has made a positive impact through innovative use of its brand power.

I had the pleasure of talking to Blake about his ideas and experiences as a social entrepreneur. I started by asking him about how TOMS started.
I started TOMS after a trip I took to Argentina in 2006. I noticed that many of the locals wore shoes that I learned were *alpargata*. I also noticed that in rural villages there were many children who were without shoes and how that was affecting their daily lives. I had to come up with a way to help and knew that relying on donations alone was not a sustainable solution, so I used my knowledge of business to come up with an idea. The result was a for-profit business model that empowers customers to help children through their purchases. For every pair of shoes purchased, a new pair is given to a child in need—One for One.

You've had great success with TOMS, but I've also read that you've made some of the typical mistakes that other entrepreneurs make. For example, "putting too many butts in too many seats." What do you mean by that, and what key mistakes should other entrepreneurs try to avoid making?
TOMS started in my Venice apartment with a simple idea, a lot of passion, and a solid mission—to use business to improve lives. We grew so quickly over the first 6 years, and we had moments where we saw the challenges

of balancing the rapid growth of a small company with remaining true to the *why* of TOMS. I learned that it's so important to keep our mission at the heart of everything we do, and I encourage the next generation of social entrepreneurs to keep that passion and focus.

Typically, when startups grow, they begin to experience the problems associated with traditional corporations— for example, slow decision-making and infighting. Have you experienced these too, and how did you solve them?

There have been plenty of challenges as TOMS has grown over the years. Like most companies, you have to understand how best to structure your teams and bring experience and leadership to guide the next phases. I don't believe this is something you "solve" but continue to learn and evolve from. Finding the right leaders for your organization is a big factor; and for us that really means evaluating them based on the experience they bring to the table but also how they fit into our culture.

In 2015, you stepped down as the CEO of TOMS—after 9 years. Why?

I realized I needed both professional and financial backing in order to keep the company moving forward. It was a long process that I put a lot of thought into. I was really fortunate to be able to fund the growth of TOMS in the early days, so I never had to rely on investors. As the sole owner, it caused me a lot of stress to not have partners to rely on to make big decisions. In order for me to be a creative innovator for our company and focus on the things I do well, such as connecting with our Giving Partners and collaborating with our design and marketing teams,

I needed to allow a really amazing CEO to run the company and be the business leader of TOMS.

What is the *why* of TOMS?

The *why* of TOMS has been and always will be about using business to improve lives. TOMS started as a business to help create a better tomorrow and encourages our tribe to be a part of the movement.

Please explain your One for One approach to readers that have never heard about this before.

When I came up with the TOMS business model, I wanted giving to be very straightforward and easy to digest. For every TOMS product you purchase, TOMS will help a person in need—One for One. It began with giving shoes and has since expanded to helping restore sight, offering safe water, supporting the training for and distribution of safe birth kits, providing bullying prevention training and services, and finally providing solar light. All of this is made possible by our TOMS consumers and the Giving Partners we work with, who are nonprofit organizations on the ground in the regions in which we give.

Does the One for One approach really help people or does it risk becoming another example of a capitalist's fly-by philanthropy?

We are constantly learning and challenging ourselves to enhance how we use business to improve lives. TOMS is mindful of the impact we have on the regions in which we give. We check in with our Giving Partners to get their feedback on how we can improve.

Following our findings, in 2013, we challenged ourselves to help create jobs and build industry by producing a portion of our Giving Shoes in the regions in which we give them. We now employ locals in factories in Ethiopia, Vietnam, India, and Kenya.

"Giving is our future," you say. What about the people who prefer not to give and just live their normal lives. Are they bad people, then—not part of the future?

TOMS has inspired many other companies to incorporate giving into their business model and that is something I'm incredibly proud of. I hope we continue to encourage others to use their platforms to do more good in this world, as I believe we all have a responsibility to do so.

Why do we need social entrepreneurship in the world?

There is a responsibility for businesses to step up and use their reach, assets, and influence for good. But this is more than a responsibility; it's also simply good business. As the world continues to shift, it is becoming increasingly clear that you can no longer do well without doing good.

You're a big believer in traveling while you are young. Why do young people need these travel experiences?

Traveling is so important because it allows a person to experience different cultures. Having material objects matters far less than many of us are led to believe. There is so much beauty in the human condition and in the spirit of the people we come in contact with every day.

Although difficult, it's important to witness what others go through in poverty-stricken regions so we can better understand their needs for basic necessities such as water, food, health care, and so on. I don't believe there is anything more meaningful than making a connection with a person—a child—and sharing their emotions with them. I cherish these moments and the experiences I've shared with all the people I've met while traveling.

You've started investing in very interesting social startups such as Owlet, Cotopaxi, and Laxmi. Can you tell us some more about some of these startups and why you've also started becoming an impact investor?

Through the TOMS Social Entrepreneurship Fund, we've invested in 15 for-profit businesses with purpose at their core. These companies range from Rubicon, a tech startup dubbed "the Uber for trash" that is disrupting the waste and recycling industries, to Artlifting, an online marketplace for artists to sell their artwork and get back on their feet. I am committed to reinvesting in purpose-driven entrepreneurs with innovative ideas to help support others that are using business to improve lives.

Where in the world do we need social entrepreneurship the most currently?

I have recently become interested in the difference between an *entrepreneur* and someone with an *entrepreneurial spirit*. We need business leaders, founders, and entrepreneurs to harness the power of business for good. But we also need all people to bring an entrepreneurial spirit into their lives—to lead with purpose and to have the courage to imagine things that do not yet exist.

How can social entrepreneurs benefit from new disruptive technologies such as 3D printing, artificial intelligence, drones, and so on?

There has been such a gigantic growth spurt in technology since TOMS started in 2006. We have seen firsthand the benefits of the internet, particularly in social media. When we first launched, platforms such as Facebook were essential to building the brand and sharing the details of our movement. We have always had a minimal marketing budget due to our giving, so we rely on our community to help us spread the word. Technology really helped us share our story with our tribe, who then turned into the best form of marketing by posting on social media.

In 2015, we created a virtual reality giving trip so now our community is able to observe a shoe-giving trip in Peru. It allows them to experience giving and to see how their shoe purchase directly helps a child. This use of technology allows our consumers to establish a deeper connection with TOMS. I hope the continued evolution of technology inspires entrepreneurs to think differently in order to drive positive change in the world.

NAVEEN JAIN
Where was the entrepreneurial dinosaur when we needed him?

Naveen Jain (India) is an entrepreneur and philanthropist driven to solve the world's biggest challenges through innovation. He is the founder of several successful companies including Viome, Bluedot, TalentWise, Intelius InfoSpace and Moon Express, where he is currently chairman.

When I'm listening to Naveen Jain describing his plan to create big business on the moon, it's hard for me to grasp that he was once a poor child in India.

Today, Naveen is a billionaire and a very successful entrepreneur. His own recipe for success is, among other things, not knowing much and not being very good at anything. To me, that sounds like the opposite of what business life normally requires, yet Naveen isn't joking, and his track record proves that he is not wrong either. After all, the young boy that grew up in poverty in India is today changing the world as we know it and has Sir Richard Branson and Google founder Larry Page as two of his good personal friends.

Naveen, I find it so inspiring that you have used entrepreneurship not only to change your own living conditions but also to change the lives of millions of other people. So I'm curious, what do you actually mean when you tell me that it's important not to know too much?

When you're really good at something, you have a tendency to only be able to improve it a little bit.

We see this all the time in companies with great skills and experience that still lose market shares to fast-growing startups, because the people in the old-thinking companies might be skilled, but they are also trapped by all of their knowledge in a particular field and only manage to produce incremental innovation, not radical or disruptive innovation.

On the other hand, when you don't know very much about a particular field, you're truly able to challenge it. This forces you to ask all the curious questions that children love to ask—those we sometimes call "stupid questions" but which are often brilliant and eye opening, because the person asking them is genuinely curious.

In my own case and career, I've never started two companies in the same industry. I'm not really an expert or guru in any particular field, but what I am is an entrepreneur, and what I love to do is challenge the status quo in industries that I become interested in or fascinated by.

You often hear that entrepreneurs are the kind of people who view the glass as half full rather than half empty. Do you agree?

No. To me, entrepreneurship is not about being overly optimistic. If you're too optimistic, you risk making bad decisions, because you think that everything you do will succeed.

The reality is the opposite. Entrepreneurs fail all the time. The challenge is not to avoid failing but to fail fast and cheap. So to me, entrepreneurship is about asking the question, is this glass worth filling?

Nice metaphor. A bit like Simon Sinek, who has also written an article for this book and who talks about starting with *why*—meaning what is your cause, what is your belief, why does your organization exist?

Is that a relevant comparison?

Yes absolutely. When I start new companies, I always start with *why*, and I combine this with thinking big. I call it *moonshot* thinking.

Moonshot thinking is about solving big problems that are worth solving. If you manage to do so, you become highly successful—both when it comes to your feeling of meaningfulness and to your bank account.

I never aim to solve problems that effect less than 100 million people in the world and preferably more. This might seem like too big a challenge to give yourself, but in fact, big problems are often not more difficult to solve than the smaller ones.

So, if this is in fact the case, and you're going to spend thousands of hours on your project no matter what, why not aim for the moon to begin with?

As I've understood your latest business venture, aiming for the moon is no longer just a metaphor for you but to be understood literally and as a potentially lucrative business opportunity for you.

Yes, that is true. My company Moon Express is about going to the moon, not like the United States did many years ago for scientific purposes but with a business intention.

The moon is a potential treasure chest that has vast amounts of iron ore, water, rare earth minerals, and precious metals, as well as carbon, nitrogen, hydrogen, and helium-3, a gas that can be used in future fusion reactors to provide nuclear power without radioactive waste. Experts concur that the value of these resources is in the trillions of dollars.

The moon can also serve as a fuel depot station for interplanetary space exploration. It has massive amounts of ice (H_2O) trapped on the lunar poles that can be used for rocket fuel.

The moon is big business because of its metals?

Yes, but not only this. It's also the possibility to develop a multiplanet society for us humans. Think about what would happen if a large asteroid hit earth. Most likely, we would all die—become extinct overnight.

Currently, we don't have any strategy or action plan for dealing with this threat, which might not be happening in the very near future but could do so in the generations to come.

When we're not addressing this, we're acting like the dinosaurs did millions of years ago. However, unlike the dinosaurs, we're able to act in a more reflective and entrepreneurial way. I mean,

Where was the entrepreneurial dinosaur when they needed him?

A multiplanet society. Wow! Again, I have to remind the readers that you grew up in a poor family in India. You were curious, wanted to fill glasses worth filling, and now you're talking about reinventing the moon for humans. Does this also mean that we will see regular people like myself traveling to the moon in the future—not only billionaires?

Yes, of course. Think about the word *honeymoon*. Instead of going to Paris for a week, why not give your new husband or wife an actual honeymoon?

The moon has always had romantic connotations, and who knows if we're not also going to disrupt the whole diamond industry with Moon Express. I mean, who would want something so boring as a diamond when you can give your wife an actual and beautiful rock from the moon?

I think in Scandinavia, where I was born and raised, this sounds fascinating on one side but also overwhelming. I mean … Going to the moon and creating a business out of it? It sounds like a sci-fi movie rather than something you would ever be able to do as a Dane.

Denmark might be a small country, but that is really just an excuse. In today's world, distance doesn't exist. There are no geographical boundaries and everyone is available to you, if your business idea and business model is good enough.

For example, you and I didn't know each other just 1 month ago, and now we're Skyping and emailing about entrepreneurship, innovation, and disruption. So the world has gotten so small, and this makes it even more meaningful to think big.

I'm very curious about how we can train young people to become entrepreneurs, like we are. Some people in my home country claim that the education system is broken. Do you agree?

No, I don't actually. The education system works precisely as it was designed to work. The problem is that the world has changed so drastically, but the way we educate people hasn't.

Our education system was developed for an industrial era, when we could teach certain skills to our children and they would be able to use these skills for the rest of their lives, working productively in an industry. We are now living in a fast-paced technological era, when every skill that we teach our children becomes obsolete in 10–15 years due to exponentially growing technological advances. Meanwhile, new categories of jobs are being created because of these technological advances.

It's hard to imagine that half the jobs that exist today didn't exist 25 years ago.

So our education system today uses the mass production–style manufacturing process of standardization. We are using the same process to teach our kids today, grouping them by their date of manufacturing (i.e., age). Once a year, we use standardized testing to see if they are ready to move to the next grade of an education-advanced assembly line. How do we then rethink this?

Rethinking education starts with embracing our individuality. Our life experiences are very different from one and other, and yet we seem to think everyone of us can learn the same way. Some of us learn experientially, while others are more attracted to logical or conceptual learning. Why are we limiting ourselves to one format or curriculum when we know that each individual is going to learn differently? Further, why are we advancing children to the next level, or grade, on an annual basis, as opposed to when each is ready?

Just think of the opportunities we can unlock by making education as addictive as a video game. This type of experiential, addictive learning improves decision-making skills and increases the processing speed and spatial skills of the brain.

You're a frontrunner in the moon race, but I understand that you and your team are also trying to disrupt things within the health industry.

You're talking about my company Viome, which by the way is another example of an industry that I knew absolutely nothing about before I started working in it.

When we started Viome, the most important thing when founding the team was not skills but trust. This is also one of the key findings that I would like to pass on to other entrepreneurs: the importance of hiring great and skilled people that you really *trust* and *like*. Those are the two keywords.

In Viome, we're curious about why people get sick and how we can control this in the future.

What we have discovered is that genetics play a very small role in our complex human body. Even identical twins can turn out very differently, and when we give people the same kind of drugs, they work differently on the individual.

At Viome, we believe that this is due to the fact that our body is in fact only 10% human and 90% microbacteria. Our body is in this sense a climate, and while there are only 20,000 genes in our human DNA, there are 10 million genes in our gut. We need to understand this complexity better.

Historically, we have believed that the causes of Parkinson's, depression, and so on are primarily neurological or originate in the brain, but recent research indicates that depression's root cause may be directly related to bacteria found in the gut.

Doctors and nutritionists have always known there is a connection between the brain and the gut, but we understand the gut better now, and it seems like the gut has a mind of its own called the *enteric nervous system.*

If we're right about these assumptions, and if we manage to crack the code, Viome has the potential to profoundly impact the medical field and be a major step forward in effectively treating and possibly curing people plagued by depression, Parkinson's, and other diseases. While changing a person's bacteria is still a stretch for doctors, it is easier and more straightforward than trying to change an individual's genes.

Last question to you Naveen: Going to the moon and solving life-threating diseases: is this big money or big impact for you?

It's both. They are not each other's opposites but should instead be closely linked. The billionaires of the future are the people who manage to solve problems for billions.

And at the end of the day, everyone reading this article could become one of them. However, money shouldn't be your key motivating factor. To find your true passion, instead ask yourself the following questions:

What if I had billions of dollars and everything that I wanted in life? What would I do then?

Find your answer and follow it!

PASCAL FINETTE
Work is love made visible

Pascal Finette (United States) heads up the Startup Program at Singularity University, where he grows startups tackling the world's most intractable problems leveraging exponential technologies. He has previously started a number of technology companies and used to work as head of eBay's Platform Solutions Group in Europe and created Mozilla's accelerator program WebFWD.

"May you live in interesting times."

Chinese proverb

This (somewhat liberally translated) Chinese proverb is something you hear often in Silicon Valley these days. Some say it is a curse. Regardless, nobody denies its truth when it comes to the change technology brings to our world.

Driven by the exponentially accelerating rate of technological progress we now have (literally) supercomputers in our pockets, can access the world's information at our fingertips, can sequence genes in our kitchen labs, and 3D print prototypes on our desktops. Gordon Moore's 50-year-old prediction that "the number of transistors in a dense integrated circuit doubles approximately every two years" (know commonly as *Moore's law*) holds up to this day and has long spilled over into other technologies and industries: your iPhone 10 has 1000 times the computational power of a Cray 1 supercomputer from the mid-1970s at about 1/50,000th of the cost—a staggering 50 million times price/performance improvement. Sequencing the human gene took us a

decade and $2.7 billion at the beginning of the 21st century. Today it takes us mere hours and costs less than $1000. And solar energy reached parity in its price/performance ratio to conventional sources of energy like coal—turning a scarce natural resource into something that will be abundantly available at little to no cost in the near-term future.

Experts will gladly tell you that computational power is already abundant, as is storage of all that data our connected systems produce. Sequencing our genome will be close to free within the next 10 years or so. And you will soon pay a small flat fee for being connected to the electric grid but not pay for the actual electrons anymore.

All this progress, at an ever-increasing pace, creates a wealth of new opportunities and disrupts existing markets faster and more forceful than ever before. Ray Kurzweil formulated this in the *law of accelerating returns*: once an industry becomes information enabled it moves on an exponential curve. Thus finding industries that are not yet information enabled (and there are plenty) and bringing these into the information age is one of the most promising business ideas these days.

"We shall require a substantially new manner of thinking if mankind is to survive."

Albert Einstein

At the same time humanity faces pressing and severe problems.

The United Nations predicts that by 2050 our planet will be populated by 9 billion people, which makes food supply a fundamental issue. Today, with about 7.2 billion people living on Earth, we technically have enough food; it is just not equally distributed (which is by no means an easy problem to solve). To feed the projected number of people, we need to grow our agricultural output by 2% year over year. Over the last few decades, we grew output by 1%, which makes one look at the current GMO debate through a very different lens.

Global Warming is already a major contributor to unpredictable and often devastating changes in weather patterns. A large number of experts suggest that by the turn of the century the sea levels will rise by as much as 2 meters. Whole countries such as Bangladesh will be flooded, should we see such a dramatic rise of our oceans. This will result in a mass movement of people as they flee to higher ground. If you want to get a taste of what this looks like, just look at the Syrian refugee crisis in the European Union.

Or take water: without access to clean drinking water, most other interventions, such as better learning tools, access to electricity, or economic opportunities, are moot. And despite technology being available to make even the most polluted water potable, more than 800 million people globally don't have access to clean drinking water.

All these, and many other, challenges are large-scale, often intertwined, complex, and pressing. And technology, particularly the technologies that move on an exponentially accelerating curve, can and almost certainly will be our best tool to solve these grand global challenges.

"The reasonable man adapts himself to the world; the unreasonable one persists in trying to adapt the world to himself. Therefore all progress depends on the unreasonable man."

George Bernard Shaw

Let me introduce you to my friend Nithya Ramanathan. Nithya teaches computer science at UCLA. A few years ago, Nithya started to fixate on a problem that affects millions of people, mostly children, worldwide: spoiled vaccines.

Most vaccines require proper cooling and handling on their journey from point of production to consumption. They need to be kept at a specific temperature without too much variance. This logistic chain is called the *cold chain*. And 75% of vaccines in the developing world show signs of freezing, with an estimated one-fourth to one-third of all vaccines that are administered being ineffective.

Nithya, together with a small team, developed an internet-connected temperature sensor that travels with the vaccine fridge through the cold chain. Constantly measuring the temperature and sending information about irregularities to both the nurse and doctor who are administering the vaccine as well as cloud-based software, Nithya's device provides, for the first time, not only real-time insights into the status of an individual batch of vaccines but also an aggregated view into where the problems typically occurs.

The device is now used in six countries; in three states in India alone there are now 11,000 devices in the field, saving the lives of millions of babies each year. And trust me, Nithya has barely just begun.

The remarkable thing about Nithya's solution is that her device is incredible simple: by leveraging a readily available *exponential* technology—a cheap, $30, Chinese-manufactured Android smartphone combined with a tiny bit of simple, custom hardware, a temperature sensor, and a bit of software—Nithya's team have built the most successful intervention in the field today.

"Work is love made visible. The goal is not to live forever; the goal is to create something that will."

Kahlil Gibran

Here's the reason why I am telling you all this: everybody can do this. Everybody can be Nithya, get up, assemble a small team, pick a big, hairy problem, and tackle it. Even if you are not a software developer, hardware hacker, or bio-engineer, I am confident that you know people who are.

Collectively, we are creating a world of technological abundance—readily available, cheap, and easy to use. It is on us to use it in the best possible way. It is on us to ask ourselves, What does it take to make the problem go away?

THE BEST WAY TO BECOME A BILLIONAIRE IS TO HELP A BILLION PEOPLE.

Peter Diamandis

MARTIN BJERGEGAARD
Do you create from the light side or the dark side?

Martin Bjergegaard (Denmark) launched his first company on his 18th birthday and is co-founder of the company factory Rainmaking, which to date has created 25 startups, as well as being the daily "home" for over a thousand entrepreneurs in Copenhagen, London, and Berlin.

A famous Albert Einstein quotation is as follows:

"The most important decision we make is whether we believe we live in a friendly or hostile universe."

So fundamental was the wish of one of world history's greatest geniuses that his fellow beings reflect upon their relationship with existence. In the same way, I would like to invite you, dear entrepreneur, innovator, or leader, to go right back to your starting point and take a helicopter view as you read the coming few pages.

When we create, we can fundamentally move from positive feelings and experiences of the world or from negative equivalents. Whether A or B, it decides if what we create is part of the solution for the world or part of the problem.

When you look around you, you will most likely agree with me that there are many problems in the world—or challenges, if you wish. Thus, much of what has been created throughout human history has been a source of problems rather than real solutions. This applies to nations, public institutions, NGOs, businesses, and everything else.

You will undoubtedly be able to name a business, large or small, that doesn't make the world a better place—rather the contrary. Why is that? Behind this creation, this business, are some people of flesh and blood who at a point in time, long ago or recently, brought this project into the world. How they looked upon their existence then, what they felt and what they thought about it, sowed the seeds of what the business is today. How they and the people they took with them on their journey have since felt about and experienced their existence has either confirmed their starting point or adjusted it.

It is obvious that this must be the way of things, as every organization is nothing by itself; it lives only because of the people who have given it a voice and form, and who still do so. Yet we still overlook this evident fact to a very high degree. We believe that the business model, the idea, and the professional skills of the team are more important than the way the founders experience the world, seen on a profoundly personal level. We don't even have a language for talking about the latter. When I ask here whether you create on the basis of the light side or the dark side, you may perhaps think that it's an odd question. It's not improbable that you look upon the question in a completely different way than the way I mean it. And we can't even be reproached for that, because we are simply not trained to communicate on that level.

So let me you give two concrete examples of how what I call the "dark side" can look in an entrepreneur's and/or a leader's reality. The examples are hypothetical—but they are nevertheless very close to things I have experienced in reality. While I write this, I'm sending kind thoughts to those who act "darkly"—for they are fundamentally well-meaning people who do their best but who on some parameters have lost their way.

Example 1

An entrepreneur I know has many companies and is quite cynical in the way he moves their assets around between them. Sometimes he lets one of his companies go bankrupt, so the suppliers do not get their money, even though he could have paid them everything without problem. He tells himself a story that it's better that he has the money than other people have it. When I look at his actions I am sure that he is incorrect about that assumption.

Example 2

One of my acquaintances has created hundreds of jobs. He's very proud of that, but it's as if he's forgotten to ask himself what the everyday experience that he offers his colleagues is. On bad days he is stressed, absent-minded, restless. This has set the pace for an unhealthy business culture, where people do not remain because of their love of the mission and the organization but rather because the leader's fears have spread to them and they are now worried about what they would otherwise be doing.

Perhaps you will say that it is necessary to be cynical in business life. On this I beg to differ. You have a much greater potential—we all do. When you successfully eradicate fear, self-criticism, and concerns from your mind, then there are no longer any problems in being the entrepreneur or leader that you at the deeper level want to be.

One of my friends often says, "Everyone is rotten in one way or another." What he really means is that he is very frustrated by not being able to find the way out of his habit of self-criticism and a fearful mind. He does many things really well, but at the same time, he is almost chronically dissatisfied. He's restless, never sincere or spontaneously happy, and he feels he has to protect himself in a hostile world. We might have normalized such a way of being in the world, and maybe we excuse ourselves by stating that we are only human.

However, we cannot allow ourselves to be so defeatist when we take upon ourselves the task of bringing creations into this world. When we understand that the quality of our creation depends completely on the quality of our inner lives and the dialogue we have with ourselves, then we suddenly acknowledge that we have an enormous responsibility for turning on the light side in ourselves—a realization that can feel very intense when we finally get it.

The method is not to focus on resisting the dark side, as that will not work. There's an aphorism that states, "What you resist persists," and it is very true. That's also why slimming diets never work in the long run. Our focus on losing weight makes us sad or frustrated, so we eat to comfort ourselves. Perhaps not in the first couple of months, but sooner or later. When, instead, full of joy and enthusiasm, we register to take part in a long-distance race and really start to involve ourselves in the project, that's when the kilos fall off, without any feeling of sacrifice. When you turn on the light, the darkness disappears by itself. You don't have to fight it; just turn on the light.

For an entrepreneur, creator, leader, turning on the light means at least three things:

1. That your business or your project is launched with a clear mission of being part of the solution, instead of being a part of the problem. Egoism is darkness; helping your fellow beings is light.

2. That in every interaction with other people you come from a position of love, trust, and a pure intention to create, rather than from the all-too-common position of mistrust, self-obsession, manipulation, and indifference.

3. That you love yourself. Seriously. I'm not talking about being arrogant, complacent, or self-sufficient. But it is really true that you cannot love others if you don't love yourself. You must learn *never* to criticize yourself, whether in words, thoughts, or feelings. Self-criticism compromises the quality and presence that you can put into your project.

An objection I often hear is that, as an entrepreneur, you *must* be chronically dissatisfied, as that is the fuel that powers you to fight for change. If you think about it, that statement is something you've heard elsewhere and now repeat without actually having thoroughly examined it. The statement is false, like so many of the other propaganda campaigns against human nature that we more or less unconsciously participate in. The truth is that we humans are born with a creative urge. Until we learned self-criticism from the adults around us, as children we threw ourselves into all kinds of creative projects. It isn't true that we humans are fundamentally lazy and that if we don't beat ourselves into action we'll just lie on the sofa. There are plenty of people who have little initiative and strength, but that's because they've criticized and doubted themselves for far too long and have now almost given up. Perhaps they insist that they really like having a good time doing nothing, but if you pay attention to the look in their eyes, their energy, and the words they use, you will discover that behind the facade they are restless, dissatisfied, and perhaps even desperate or despairing. It's in our nature to challenge ourselves, to be curious and learn new things, to grow all the time. Being entrepreneurs and creators therefore suits us perfectly. People who create and build are generally more authentically present in life than people who demolish, maintain, or are on standby.

So far, many more have unfortunately come from the dark side than from the light side. That's why we have problems in the world. The Dalai Lama has said, "If every 8-year-old in the world is taught meditation, we will eliminate violence from the world within one generation." He's probably right about that. In the same way, I'd say that if all creators turned up the light in themselves more, if they really learned to love themselves, and if they were deeply rooted in positive thoughts and feelings, then all problems created by human beings could be eliminated in the course of a generation.

TO THE BEAUTIFUL MEANS TO BE YOURSELF. YOU DON'T NEED TO BE ACCEPTED BY OTHERS. YOU NEED TO ACCEPT YOURSELF.

Thich Nhat Hanh

RICHARD ST JOHN
Five simple ways to get super ideas

Richard St John is an award-winning communicator, success analyst, and author. He loves researching and analyzing complex subjects, then simplifying and communicating them in understandable terms. His best-selling book is *The 8 Traits Successful People Have in Common*, and his talk "8 Secrets of Success" is one of the most viewed TED talks.

Bill Gates once said, "I had an idea, founding the first microcomputer software company," and that idea was the springboard for his entire business success. One idea is often the starting point for success at anything, whether it's building a business, changing the world, or just deciding where to have lunch. So the question is, How do people come up with the super ideas that change their lives and often the world? Well, for over a decade, I've been researching, analyzing, and finding answers to that question. The good news is, there's no magic to coming up with ideas and you don't have to be artsy or "creative." Many of the world's greatest ideas come from ordinary people doing surprisingly simple things. So here are five simple ways you too can get a super life-changing idea.

1. Have a problem.

Ideas are really solutions to problems, so to come up with a super idea, it helps to have a problem. Sky Dayton told me he had a problem: "I was trying to get connected on the Internet, and I spent 80 frustrating hours with my computer, and the service people wouldn't even answer the phone. I had horrible service and a very frustrating experience. I thought, 'I can make this easy and people are going to want it [*Bing!*],' and I came up with the idea for EarthLink." A super idea made Sky a technology star and very rich at a young age.

Richard Branson had a problem when his flight to Puerto Rico was cancelled and he was stranded in the airport. To solve the problem, he phoned around and chartered a plane. Then he ran around the airport, found a blackboard, and scribbled in big letters, "Cheap flight to Puerto Rico." The other stranded passengers bought tickets, he filled the plane, and he actually ended up making a profit. Then, after the flight, a passenger said to him, "That wasn't bad. Fix up the service a little and you could be in business." [*Bing!*] And Virgin Atlantic was born.

2. Listen.

Richard listened, and keeping your ears open in everyday situations is another way to get super ideas. One day, Bernard Silver was in a grocery store when he heard the president of the store ask for help to automate grocery checkouts [*Bing!*]. Bernard got the idea for the barcode, an invention that revolutionized retail checkouts.

Beatle Ringo Starr was often getting his words mixed up, and one morning after the Beatles worked through the night, Ringo said, "Phew, it's been a hard day's night." John and Paul were listening and [*Bing!*] they got the idea for "Hard Day's Night," which became one of the most influential musical films of all time and one of the greatest songs of all time.

The first use of Botox was to treat muscle spasms, and Dr. Jean Carruthers was injecting Botox into a patient's eyelids to stop them from fluttering. The patient asked, "Why didn't you inject between my eyebrows?" Jean replied, "You don't have spasms there." The patient said, "I know, but when you treat me there I get this beautiful untroubled expression on my face." [*Bing!*] Jean got the idea to use Botox to reduce frown lines, and a whole new industry was born. Her advice: "You've got to listen to your patients, number one." And I'd say, in business you have to listen to your customers and clients, number one.

3. Look around.

Want to get a super idea that wins you the Nobel Prize? Simply keep your eyes open and look around. It worked for physicist Richard Feynman. In his book *Surely You're Joking, Mr. Feynman!*, he wrote, "I was in the [Cornell University] cafeteria and some guy, fooling around, throws a plate in the air. As the plate went up in the air I saw it wobble, and I noticed the red Cornell medallion on the plate going around. It was pretty obvious to me that the medallion went around faster than the wobbling." [*Bing!*] Richard got an idea, went away, worked out the motion of the mass particles (whatever they are), and won the Nobel Prize in physics. Gee, I look at a plate and all I see is food. He looks at a plate and wins the Nobel Prize. Now that's observation!

Ron Rice told me that looking around changed his life. He was a lifeguard sitting on a lifeguard stand at the beach, keeping an eye on swimmers, but he also looked at the suntan oil people were using and he thought, "Even with my limited chemistry knowledge, I could make something a hundred times better!" [*Bing!*] Ron got the idea for Hawaiian Tropic, a more appealing suntan lotion with an exotic coconut fragrance. It was a super idea that took him from the minimum wage lifeguard stand to an exotic beach house with Ferraris in the driveway.

So EYE-Q is often more important than IQ. As Marilyn vos Savant says, and she has one of the highest IQs ever recorded, "To acquire knowledge, one must study; but to acquire wisdom, one must observe." Or as Warren Buffett simply says, "In the end, I always believe my eyes rather than anything else."

4. Borrow ideas.

Having trouble coming up with ideas? Simply borrow someone else's idea and then build it into your own super idea. One day, Steve Jobs went on a tour of Xerox's R&D labs, and they showed him a graphical user interface (GUI), where you clicked images on the screen instead of typing complex codes. Steve said, "I was blown away with the potential of that graphical user interface." [*Bing!*] He saw a way to make computers much easier to use, rushed back to Apple, and that super idea turned into the Mac.

Ruth Handler's daughter used to play with dolls, and in the old days, dolls usually looked like infants, not adults. But then one day Ruth was on a trip to Germany, and she saw a very sleek and sexy adult doll that was actually a gag gift for men. [*Bing!*] Ruth got the idea to make a doll that looked like a woman and girls could dress her in different clothes. She brought the German doll back home to her company Mattel, and they created Barbie, the world's most popular doll. So Barbie actually started out as a tiny porn star for guys, but don't tell your kids.

5. Write it down.

When you suddenly get a super idea, the most important thing to do is simple: *Write it down right now!* Or your super idea will fly away, never to return.

Four Seasons Hotels founder Issy Sharp said to me, "If an idea comes up I will always, always, stop and make a note, wherever I am, even at dinner." He could be at dinner with President Obama and he'll still pull out his pen and paper and take notes.

Bob Dylan didn't pull his great ideas for songs out of the air. He pulled them out of a box. One day he was complimented on a song he'd written and he said, "Oh I didn't write that. The box did." Bob explained that if he was walking down the street or in a restaurant and he heard somebody say something interesting [*Bing!*], he pulled out his pen and paper and wrote the idea down. When he got home he threw the piece of paper in a box, and when he needed ideas for a new song, he just went to the box.

And if Larry Page didn't write down his ideas, there might be no Google today. He said, "When I was 23 I suddenly woke up thinking, What if we could download the whole Web and just keep the links? [*Bing!*] I grabbed a pen and started scribbling out the details and Google was born. When a really great dream shows up, grab it." But you can't grab it if you have nothing to grab it with. So I always carry paper and two pens, in case one runs out of ink, and also a small recorder. If I ever have a super idea, there's no way it will get away from me!

THERE IS ONE THING STRONGER
THAN ALL THE ARMIES IN THE
WORLD, AND THAT IS AN IDEA
WHOSE TIME HAS COME.

Victor Hugo

CAMILLA LEY VALENTIN
Starting without an idea

Camilla Ley Valentin (Denmark) is founder of the SaaS company Queue-it, which supplies an online queuing system designed to manage overload situations on websites in connection with massive end-user peaks. She also serves as the board chairman and board member of a number of IT/internet companies.

At Queue-it, we're often asked how we came up with the idea of inventing the world's first online queuing system—who invented it, when, why, and so on. I wish that the story of the invention had an exotic origin and character, but it doesn't.

The truth is that we started the team without having a concrete product idea.

In the beginning, my co-founders, Niels Henrik Sodemann and Martin Pronk, and I met in our spare time over a period of several months before we started the business. Many other companies have started in this way, so there is nothing unusual about that. Our history differs in that we actually started the process of establishing our own company without having any specific ideas outside of developing software-based cloud computing, the most important megatrend in technology we saw at the time.

So we started two parallel processes in order to move forward with ideation. One was to bind ourselves legally to ensure mutual commitment, and the other was to provide the necessary basis for agreeing on our collaboration. In concrete terms, this process comprised of three important milestones:

1. A nondisclosure agreement (NDA) in which we promised each other not to tell anyone that we were having these discussions, nor what we were discussing. As a result, all of the ideas that arose during the process are still secret, including those that we did not select.

2. A letter of intent (LOI), stating that it was our intention to start a joint company with the purpose of developing and selling a queuing system.

3. A shareholder agreement and employment agreements, which regulate our ownership structure and the agreements among us, and the agreed conditions of employment.

When setting up a company where there are several partners, it is incredibly important to get these factors sorted out before the start, and it doesn't take much to get the documents themselves finalized. The discussions that are the foundation of the final agreements do, however, take time and a fair amount of mental energy.

The other process focused on the product itself, the idea, the invention.

As mentioned, we developed the idea on the background of a set of simple but broad criteria:

- Cloud computing (software-as-a-service)

- International market potential
- New invention

With these agreements and corner flags in place, we started a relatively classical innovation process. This process is outlined in the following illustration:

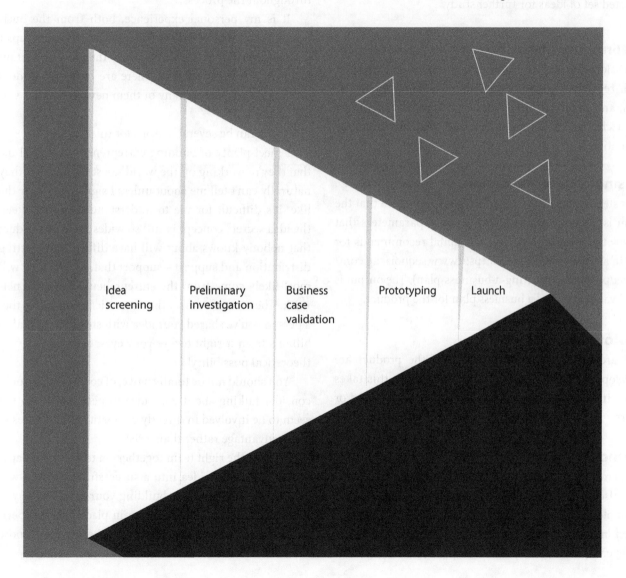

Idea screening · Preliminary investigation · Business case validation · Prototyping · Launch

Idea Screening

In the first stage there is room for all suggestions and more-or-less crazy ideas. The team reviews the ideas and reaches an agreement about which will go on to the next step. The output is a "go or no go" in order to advance a selected set of ideas for further study.

Preliminary Investigation

The selected ideas are studied further here, in particular with regard to market potential, the competitive situation, and other viability factors. The output is go/no go for a chosen idea before it goes to final business case validation.

Business Case Validation

This step results in a detailed analysis of the idea that the team is leaning toward within a set of parameters that follow the criteria that Sequoia Capital recommends for use in a business plan (see: https://www.sequoiacap.com/grove/posts/6bzx/writing-a-business-plan). The output is final validation and a business plan for the product.

Prototyping

The architecture and first version of the product are developed and validated. It is important that this takes place in collaboration with potential customers and/or users.

Launch

The product is presented to the world. In practice, this can also be done before a beta version is launched. For example, by using a teaser-site, for those who are interested in being notified when the product is available live and perhaps where they can some parts of the system.

It is necessary that the process from start to finish is approached in an iterative way, which in this situation means that an idea, after each step, can go further or start over if the findings from the step suggest. In other words, you should be ready to reject a chosen idea at any time throughout the process.

It is my personal experience, both from the businesses I am involved with and from the other startups I have observed, that the idea is rarely the most important factor in achieving success. There are many good ideas out there, and a great many of them never become a viable business.

There can be several reasons for this.

I meet plenty of budding entrepreneurs who tell me that they're working on the world's best idea, which they naturally can't tell me about unless I sign an NDA or the like. It's difficult for me to understand why this "keep the idea secret" concept is still so widespread. A product that nobody knows about will have difficulty in getting distribution and support—support that, in the start, will most likely come from the entrepreneur's personal network. There is, of course, the theoretical possibility that a person you've shared your idea with steals it and makes billions from it right before your eyes; but that is a very theoretical possibility!

You should not be totally naive, of course, but I would consider talking about your idea to people who do not seem to be involved in directly competitive businesses to be an advantage rather than a risk.

Putting the right team together—a team that is capable of turning the idea into a successful business—will be much more critical to building your business. If you have the right co-founding team in place, you'll experience that you can go far no matter whether you choose the 100% correct idea from day one.

THE SECRET OF GETTING AHEAD IS GETTING STARTED. THE SECRET OF GETTING STARTED IS BREAKING YOUR COMPLEX OVERWHELMING TASKS INTO SMALLER MANAGEABLE TASKS, AND THEN STARTING ON THE FIRST ONE.

Mark Twain

PAAVO BECKMAN
How to conquer the world without money

Paavo Beckman (Finland) has been CEO and co-founder at five entertainment and tech companies and led teams in San Francisco, New York, London, and Finland. He is an expert in startups and corporations and an evangelist of lean startup methods.

My fellow student Jussi and I were always thinking that we were going to be actual rock stars, but finally it hit us that it wasn't going to happen. So we decided to start a record label. We took student loans and together we were able to raise €1000. The office for the company consisted of Jussi's bedroom, and his bed acted as a seat for us. I was involved a lot in the music events, and soon people started thinking that our label was a lot bigger than it was. Suddenly, I was also on the boards of various music organizations.

As the income of the company was basically just coins, we started thinking about how we could compete with big record labels such as Universal, Sony, and Warner. They have heaps of money and are able to buy media space and so on. What we had was an understanding of fan communities. We decided to sign a totally unknown band and not to tell anybody about it. We didn't even try to get interviews or radio plays because the media wouldn't have cared anyway. We also decided not to print out any ads, which was an easy decision since we wouldn't have had the money for it regardless.

2005-2007

The band we signed had 19 teenage girl fans and their email addresses. Our goal was that the band will be number one on the Finnish music chart with a marketing budget of €80. We started by focusing on those 19 fans because they cared about the band. Big labels have a good understanding of distribution channels and the use of media, but we wanted to make this happen the other way around. I was the manager of the band, and with the lead singer we started to email the fans. At this time, Facebook or Twitter didn't exist. We built a story for the fans about how the band was negotiating for a record deal and told them that it was highly confidential information and needed to be kept secret. This was actually true, but the negotiating parties were the manager of the band and the record label, which meant that I would basically have been negotiating with myself. We gave the fans exclusive information, which made them feel they were special. So they ended up starting to market the band themselves. For example, the girls took toilet paper rolls from school toilets and wrote things about the band on every sheet. Then they returned them to the toilets, and every time somebody would use a sheet of toilet paper, they would see something concerning the band. Obviously, this raised a lot of questions and interest in who and what the band were.

When the first CD was released, the whole thing had evolved to a point where kids around the big cities of Finland would skip school to go and queue in front of record stores so they could get the CD. The CD jumped up to number one on the Finnish chart and sold twice as much as the number two. It was only a matter of time until the media would start contacting me asking about the band. We made a list of media outlets that we considered to be good value. For these companies, we would tell them, "Maybe we can find the time for a two-page interview." The companies that we didn't hold in high esteem we told, "We can arrange an interview for a €4000 fee." These companies had been used to getting paid by big record labels to get them to write something about their artists.

Obviously, now the media was even more interested in what was going on.

Everything that is exclusive in the world becomes valuable, even though it might not be useful in anyway, like an autograph on a record or a piece of gold.

The end game of this is pretty clear, and here are some of the titles the band won that year:

- Newcomer of the Year in what was at the time the biggest music magazine in Finland
- Best Song of the Year on the biggest radio station in Finland

- Best Music Video of the Year on a big music portal in Finland
- Young Power of the Year in the most appreciated music magazine in Finland
- Three number one singles on the hit chart

Around this time, the MySpace service had been launched, and some bands were using it, including us. Through MySpace, the band got some attention abroad too, and when some girl from Germany would write a comment on the band's MySpace, we would make personal contact with her immediately. The same thing that we were able to make happen in Finland would start all over again in Germany.

We wanted to distribute 40,000 flyers in Germany and asked the fans if there were any volunteers, and there were plenty. As we didn't have money for the flyers, we agreed with a merchandise company that they would pay and print out the flyers and their commercial would be on the backside of the flyer. After this, the fans in America contacted us and wanted to distribute some flyers too. They had already designed them and would print them out themselves. The response was "Go ahead."

Without any promoters or distributors, the band's single ended up as the whole of Europe's 65th most sold single. At this point, we made a deal and licensed the band to Sony. The future would hold a big tour in Europe at festivals and clubs. You might be asking why you haven't heard of this band called Bloodpit. During the first gig of the tour, the band started throwing fists and instruments at each other in the middle of the gig and then broke up. The band would never get together again and all the gigs had to be cancelled.

2007 onward

What if all this could be done through cell phones? For example, the lead singer could just grab the phone and send a message to the 10 most active fans in London saying, "We're coming to London and it would be great to meet up." Without any kind of understanding of the technology, we started to build the idea. We applied for the Mobile Rules competition in the United States. We were picked to be in the final 10 best applicants from around the world. Obviously, everybody else would have great videos and visuals, so we were trying to think about how to compete with these other companies. We took €50 and hired an artist to draw us a rock-themed comic. The final was held at Yahoo's headquarters in Silicon Valley, and to everybody's surprise and despite my horrible knowledge of the English language, we won the whole thing. I was told to haul ass to New York to a certain hotel and I would be picked up from there. I did as I was told, and there was a limousine waiting for me there the next day. A bit later, I had somehow gathered a couple of million in investments.

There, I was now CEO of a company called Mobile Backstage. Jussi was a product guy and he was forced to buy his first cell phone (he was quite likely the last person in Finland not to own one). We started a collaboration with one tech company, and after a year we bought their mobile communication platform and a couple of software developers from the company.

Quite soon we had as customers platinum- and gold-selling artists from the United States and United Kingdom and had offices in San Francisco, New York, London, and Helsinki. In 2012, I left the United States to move back to Finland because of my family. I hired IBM's former big data director as the new CEO. I heard that the company faced closing in 2015 because the management team and investors weren't able to agree on relocating the headquarters of the company from Europe to the United States, and finally there was only an empty company with no employees.

After moving to back to Europe, I was doing mentoring for accelerators, big corporations, and tens of startups in nine countries. That's when I realized how slow the progress is for startups in Europe, no matter how good they are. I decided to start solving those problems, and so Startup Catapult was born. Nowadays, Catapult helps international multi-billion-dollar corporations in different business sectors to find the best startups based on their needs. We scan through more than 100,000 European startups annually with the help of artificial intelligence and pick up the best ones for our corporate clients.

Top three tips for conquering the world without money

1. Focus on the people who want to be part of your thing and personalize the marketing, so those people can experience the whole journey. Give people a reason to tell stories, give them behind-the-scenes access.

2. Even in big corporations, the people in charge are just humans, so find the guy who gets excited about your thing and he will sell it to his co-workers. This isn't a story that applies to just the music business but follows certain logic that will always work when doing business with humans.

3. If you want to reach 100,000 people, focus on 100, as when you focus on 100,000, nobody will experience that this is personally for them. When you get 100 people really on your side, they will be the most powerful marketing machines you can have.

WAITING FOR PERFECT IS NEVER AS SMART AS MAKING PROGRESS.

Seth Godin

SOPHIE TRELLES-TVEDE
From bad taste to *Forbes* magazine

Sophie Trelles-Tvede (Denmark) is the co-founder of invisibobble and was named as one of Europe's 30 greatest entrepreneur talents by *Forbes*. Her products are distributed in over 70 countries and have earned her the 30 Under 30 Europe: Retail and E-Commerce prize.

My name is Sophie, and I've just turned 23 at the time of writing this. My life is quite hectic. Here are some examples of what has happened to me over the past 4 weeks.

Forbes magazine named my friend and partner Felix and me among the 2016 30 Under 30 Europe: Retail and E-Commerce award recipients, and a few days later, the Copenhagen School of Design and Technology (KEA) broadcast a TEDx Talk with me, in which I talked about entrepreneurship. This resulted in many enquiries about talks and interviews, of which we can only manage a few. In addition, I took part in a product launch in Paris, visited our production facilities in China, took legal action against a supplier in California (he withdrew his products), negotiated new distribution agreements with various companies, went Kitzbühel with some team members for a sales training, and conducted recruitment interviews with eight people.

Privately, I was with a dance troupe at the carnival in Rio, skied in St Anton, and celebrated my 23rd birthday in Switzerland. I must also admit to getting a fine for driving too close to another car. All this within the past 3 weeks, when I've only slept 5 hours a night on average.

So, yes, it's been hectic, and the main reason for this is probably that I'm an entrepreneur!

Why all this?

Well, it started 3 months after I, as an 18-year-old, began a degree course in business management at the University of Warwick in England. In reality, my plan then was as follows:

1. Use the 3 years of my bachelor course "to find myself"—that is, find out what I really wanted and get some professional knowledge, of course.

2. When I'd found myself, I'd take a master's degree in whatever subject I was passionate about—whether it was marketing, finance, or something completely different.

3. Then get a super job in a consultancy, for example, as a springboard to a career.

4. Finally, get a good job in a well-reputed business where, after a few years, I could become responsible

for a product or a branch and thereafter perhaps start my own business in a branch that I fully understood.

I still believe today that this plan would have given me a good and productive life; it has done so for many others. But that's not what happened.

The reason why things didn't go as planned is a little bizarre. The cause was that, a few weeks after my studies at Warwick had started, I was invited to a "bad taste party," and as part of my outfit—which should express resolutely bad taste—I used an old-fashioned telephone cord as a hair band.

A hair band tends to tug on the hair and can give you a headache, probably because the small muscles in the scalp pull in the opposite direction, and in addition it leaves a kink in the hair when you remove it. Most people with long hair know this.

However, when I woke up the morning after the party, I noticed that although I was still wearing the telephone cord in my hair, I didn't have a headacheas I usually do when I tie up my hair. When I took it out, I realized I didn't have a kink in my hair as I usually got with other hair ties. I looked at the telephone cord perplexed—and then it hit me. Because the telephone cord has a different shape to hair ties, it puts an uneven pressure on the hair, thus not leaving a kink. I therefore asked myself if making hair ties designed after old-fashioned telephone cords would be a good idea … which is when I rang Felix, the friend I mentioned, who was also 18 at that time, and who was studying at the University of Bath. I told him about my strange observation and idea, and I asked him, "Don't you want to be a part of that?" Initially, he thought it sounded silly, but he and I had both been feeling a bit empty from sitting in a classroom all day, so we'd already discussed that, if we could get a good business idea, then

we should consider it seriously. We'd actually talked about it several times. So after a little more palaver, I was happy he said, "Yes, let's try it!" And so we got going, and invisibobble was founded.

The first tasks were really quite easy, and we enjoyed doing them, because we were full of expectations. For instance, firstly we had to find a name for the company. And then a logo, which we did ourselves in Photoshop, but that meant we had to invest some of our savings in the software. After that, we had to find a factory in China that could make some demo hair ties. And so it went on with packaging, pricing policy, and other things.

While other students went to plenty of parties, Felix and I sat every evening Skyping about all these things. Often we met at each other's universities and worked on the project together.

When we'd got the demo hair ties made, we showed them to various distributors, and we got a lot of help here because Felix's brother Daniel and his friend Niklas together had a company called New Flag, which already sold hair brushes (Tangle Teezer) in Germany, Austria, and Switzerland, and therefore had many contacts in the branch. Thus they already had distribution in a couple of countries, and we had a new product. It was like a hand-in-glove situation, and New Flag started to mention our product at their own sales meetings. In the meantime, Felix and I sat in our rooms and packed and sent our products for free in hopes of getting leads. I can remember a plethora of trips to the post office.

One of the most fantastic moments of my life was when we got our first order. I can easily imagine that this may sound weird to many people, because the most fantastic moment in one's life must surely have something to do with love or the universe or something like that, and in the end I suppose that is true. But when you start a business in a student dorm room, and one day, suddenly, there is a large, serious company that couldn't care less about you as a person but apparently is more than willing to buy your product, then it feels really wild. Imagine! They're ignoring that you're 18 and living in a room at university! "They consider us equals!" I thought in astonishment. "They're taking us quite seriously." And that's what Felix thought as well. We were ecstatic.

When I took my final exams at Warwick 3 years later, we had 22 employees and distribution via retail chains in about 40 countries. By the time, after another 2 years, I turned 23, we were majority owned by New Flag, and our organization had grown to over 100 people, of whom 25 worked solely with packing and sending the products. Sitting in our dorm rooms and packing hair ties was suddently a thing of the past. Now there were pallets four floors high, forklift trucks and lorries. That was how my life became what I described at the start of this short story—very hectic, but also wildly exciting.

So what have we learned from this that we haven't already been told at our universities?

Here are 10 of our most important observations:

1. Because of crowdsourcing, cloud computing, shareware, Skype, and so on, the cost of starting a business is remarkably small today; at least it was for Felix and me. Our overall initial investment was about $4000—money that we'd earned as skiing instructors while at school. Of course that was a lot of money for us then, but if we hadn't used the money on this project, it would surely have been spent on drinks. I actually calculated that we could

have bought 1350 vodka Red Bulls for the money, but that wouldn't have given us the same lasting pleasure.

2. You don't have to be an expert in your field to get success. Outsiders obviously have some handicaps, but on the other hand, they think more originally, which can give great advantages. For instance, Felix and I began to distribute hair ties to sectors that had never sold hair ties before.

3. A product doesn't necessarily have to be complex to be successful. Many of the biggest business ideas are very simple, and the advantage of something simple is partly that you can build the business very quickly if it works, and partly that the adventure is quite cheap if it's a flop.

4. Who you choose as a partner is really decisive. Felix and I knew each other from many years at school together, and we therefore knew that we could rely completely on each other's abilities and dedication. It worked. On the other hand, we quickly found a company that offered exclusive distribution in Scandinavia, which impressed us so much that we didn't check their true strength on the market fully. That was an expensive mistake.

5. Keep your expenses down. In the beginning we sent everything by airmail, but when at the end of the year we calculated what our expenses had actually been used on, we realized that this item ate the largest part by far of our potential profits. The conclusion is that you should not only be cost-conscious when there's a crisis; you must be cost-conscious every day, all the time. Even if you don't have an

aggressive competitor right behind you, you must act as if you do.

6. Notwithstanding the above, we learned that if you, like us, achieve global distribution and travel a great deal, then it pays to fly business class, as you can get a good night's sleep. It saves time and hotel expenses, and most airports have showers.

7. I know that network effects in parts of the software and media industries may make it unnecessary to protect all of its intellectual property. However, in other industries—like ours—there are hardly any network effects, and therefore you must protect your intellectual property quickly and efficiently. We only learned this along the way, but now we are masters of it. However, our lives would have been easier if we had fully understood this from the start.

8. Don't give the most prominent titles to the first people you recruit. If you do, you'll have a problem if you, like us, become much larger and can recruit more experienced and competent people later.

9. There are many disadvantages to being a small company, but one advantage may be that you can act with the speed of lightning. For example, do not let emails go unanswered for several days. Reply to everything at lightning speed. Use your smartphone for this if you're not at your computer. And send, for example, minutes of meetings to participants within an hour of the end of the meeting.

10. There will never be a time in your life when the personal risk of starting a company is smaller than when you're a student. As a student you have no large recurring expenses, no family responsibilities, and no CV that can be ruined. If things go awry, you can just finish your studies and get on with a traditional career. If it goes well, it'll probably be hectic, but also great fun.

ANDREAS EHN
Music for everyone

Andreas Ehn (Sweden) is a serial entrepreneur and was the first employee and CTO at Spotify. He currently works at Wrapp, where he is both the co-founder and CTO. Ehn is a board member and angel investor in several companies, and he is frequently hired as an advisor by promising internet startups and venture capital funds.

In 2008, the world got a new music streaming service named Spotify. It was developed in Stockholm, Sweden, and provided digital rights management–protected content from record labels and media companies.

It may have started out as a local thing, but the freemium service quickly expanded. Today, Spotify has more than 140 million monthly active users and over 50 million paying subscribers.

I had the pleasure of meeting up with Andreas Ehn, who was Spotify's first employee and CTO. Andreas was responsible for the product and platform architecture as well as hiring a world-class engineering team, of which many have gone on to become successful entrepreneurs on their own.

After Spotify, Andreas founded Wrapp—a mobile online-to-offline customer acquisition service for bricks-and-mortar retailers that raised money from prominent investors including Atomico and Greylock (with Niklas Zennström and Reid Hoffman joining the board).

Many people talk about disruption and how to disrupt markets. Did Napster disrupt the music industry or did Spotify?
Neither, I believe.

Technology disrupted the industry. The massive-scale file sharing of Napster completely changed the dynamics in the business and completely revolutionized music online. Ultimately, it forced the labels to consider new business models, and this enabled the rise of streaming—which was led by Spotify.

In the beginning with Napster, you could access music very conveniently, but no one was really paying for it. Then iTunes launched, but as I understand, you guys didn't really look at them for inspiration?
True. Spotify did not have the same mindset as iTunes. Everyone else had tried to launch a music service and just looked at the commercial landscape of other licensed services. Our background was not music or consumption, because we were computer science graduates with hacker mentalities, so we focused on file sharing as our main source of inspiration.

We were all pirating music for our own needs, so we set out to build a commercial service that would be better than piracy. The key element was that the price point had to be zero, and we created an ad-funded solution. That strategy took a long time for the labels to accept, so we didn't launch commercially until 2 years after, we started working on the service.

And no venture companies would invest in you guys in the beginning?

No. We were lucky enough to have founders who had built and sold businesses before. Martin had built a highly successful marketing company named Tradedoubler, and Daniel had in fact sold his company to Tradedoubler. That is how they got to know each other, and that is how we got enough money to finance the first couple of years, when we earned absolutely nothing.

I've seen you discussing this dilemma about being perfect versus good enough. Meaning how good should a product or service be before you introduce it to the marketplace. Where is your take on this today?

I think that my mindset has shifted over the years. I started with a classical engineering mindset—meaning that everything should be really well built before we launch it.

Today, I think that I've realized that only the market really gives you the true answers, so you should ship sooner. Time and time again it's been shown impossible to know in advance.

You mention that you were not really looking at the existing services to compete with. What was your mission then?

We entered an industry where the record labels fundamentally wanted music to be expensive. They would rather sell something expensive to fewer people; before, their mindset was that music is an art form, and art costs money.

Our approach was to change the fundamentals of music online. We introduced a free model that people still to this day want us to shut down.

We entered into a market where there were no viable online business models. People had more or less stopped buying CDs, so we had to convince the record labels that Spotify was the way to go in this bleeding market. It took time, but we started locally and from there started signing national and global deals.

If Napster had never disrupted the music industry, would we ever have had a Spotify too?

I think something else would have existed anyway. Napster and Spotify were natural children of their time. People were already pirating things online, so the next obvious step was to build some sort of sustainable and viable business model around this.

What was the biggest strength of Spotify as a company?

It was and still is the focus on user experience, I believe.

Today, Spotify is moving more toward becoming a media company, and in fact I think this is the biggest threat to the business model right now—risking to lose having tech at the core of everything you do.

Spotify managed to attract all the best engineers, because we were not a conventional music label or media company but a tech company that focused on user experience and technical skills among our staff members.

You left Spotify after having worked there for some years, and then you moved away from Sweden. Why this desire to leave your home country?

For different reasons. First of all, I'm a very curious person. I have started on a personal education project, where I want to learn more about the world and understand it better. For this reason, I've set up a framework for myself where I should live in 10 different countries for the next 5 years—so 6 months in each place. My goal is to get to know these places. Get to know the people. Get to know the cities, the startups, and so on. And also be doing some investments there.

Do people that have big dreams need to leave their home country?

Not necessarily, but for instance, living in San Francisco in the United States or in Shenzen in China will just give you completely different opportunities than most places. You are in the epicenter of tech innovation, and just being there and working there makes you bump into things and people that you would never do in, for instance, my home town of Stockholm.

I'M NOT AN INVENTOR. I JUST
WANT TO MAKE THINGS BETTER.

Daniel Ek, Spotify

THOR ANGELO
Don't underestimate the "product–market fit" phase

Thor Angelo (Denmark) is a serial entrepreneur, investor, and startup adviser. Angelo has a background as co-founder of the international growth company LanguageWire, and today he is involved in interesting companies such as OrderYOYO, MyMonii, GroupCam, and Shoptagr.

Over the past 3 years I've seen more than 300 different pitches. I've helped 50 go further, some with just a bit of advice, others with a network and connections, and I've helped about 20 of them with investments, time, and execution.

My advice on and help with these ideas and startups and to the people behind them are starting to form a pattern. There are several things that I say to them all again and again—things that everyone needs to hear.

The most important of them is, Don't underestimate the *product–market fit* phase.

Short introduction

In 1999, we were three young lads with an idea in a PowerPoint presentation, and we started the company LanguageWire. We all had master's degrees in business economics, so we were thorough, we'd learnt how to write reports, and we'd used 6 months on making a 60-page business plan. It was a complete waste of time; we never followed it.

But (later) we were very successful and had offices in eight countries, over 100 employees, almost DKK 150 million in annual turnover, and were among the 30 largest translation companies in the world when I made my exit in 2012.

What made the difference was when we started to get customers and helped them translate. In that way, we adjusted our product and business. As the Lean Startup movement manifests, it's a matter of starting and *getting five customers*. It can't be said often enough: *Get five customers. Now. Today.*

It's not until you get customers that your idea is really tested. Your mother-in-law or a good friend will always say to you, "What a super-good idea! It sounds really wild." But a customer who's going to pay for your service or product will always be 100% honest; will he pay money for what you're offering him? Forget your mother-in-law and get five customers. That's the *only* way to get your idea verified. If the idea can't fly, then it's a matter of finding that out quickly, so you don't waste 2 years in the basement and only then face reality.

When you meet your customers you will with 99% probability adjust your concept so it better suits your customers' wishes. Lean Startup calls this a *pivot*; that is, you adjust something in your concept and try again. It can be the price, the product, the target group—whatever it takes for you to get a way in. And that is *precisely* what I've acquired enormous respect for over time in my work with startups: get your idea tested on real customers now! Then you'll be in a position to adjust your product/concept so you hit the market's bull's-eye 100%.

(*Note*: One of the Lean Startup principles is that processes and products may be manual and work heavy at first—as long as you do have a plan/idea to be able to automate them later. So go out and *be* the product at the start. Do everything manually in the beginning; later, you can develop the software or buy the machines or the cheap labor that can make you more efficient.)

One of my most successful startups, which right now is flying with over 30 employees (28 recruited in just 5 months) and a total investment of over DKK 5 million to date, has used 18 months to find the correct product–market fit. In that period, we were only one or two people employed part-time. We have changed the concept fundamentally once (large pivot) and changed target groups twice (medium-sized pivots). That has also meant that we now have a different, third target group than when we started 2 years ago—an extremely instructive observation when you consider how sure we were about our concept 2 years ago. But a lot of work with potential customers has led us through these three pivots and to where we are today, with the perfect concept and target group.

LanguageWire started back in 1999 as a portal for the translation branch. At our investor meetings, we were already having to change the concept to a trading platform for translation services. No one believed in the idea of a portal. We started with the trading platform concept

and got customers. Upload the document for translation, get some offers from translators from around the world, and choose the offer you like the best. But after 6 months and the first 200 jobs, we had to change the concept as our customers couldn't be bothered to trade on the platform. They wanted more service. So we made a large pivot and changed the concept to one where we were the translation company, running the trading platform in the background. It worked better and we had more success.

After 2 years we had to change our product. We launched an extra product, so there were now two different qualities to choose between. Before we had just a translation, but after 2 years we had a cheap, low-quality translation and the more expensive, high-quality translation. That was the last large pivot we made, so after 2 or 3 years with three pivots, the concept was in place and we were ready for growth.

A third example is another of my startups, BillyTracker, which in theory is a fantastic idea: small GPS gadgets for small children (before they get mobile phones), so you can see where they are via an app on your smartphone. Relax completely at the playground or in the woods; your son is just over there. It's a concept we've worked with for 3 years now, but we still haven't found its perfect product–market fit. Who is the perfect target group? Children? Dogs? Your wife/husband? And what is the perfect user situation? Holidays? Trips? Everyday life? We're still testing everything with our customers before we step on the accelerator and go all-out with the team.

Another piece of advice I may just squeeze in here is that I'm one of the few business angels/startup people who *do not* recommend that you quit your job and spend all your time on a startup in the idea phase. Finding a correct product–market fit takes time. Book five meetings with potential customers, hold them, and 2 months will most likely have passed before they have all had the time needed to digest the discussions. And in that period, there is *nothing* to do apart perhaps from a little product development. Forget the social media, website, and so on. They're a waste of time. The product–market fit phase can take a long time—3 years perhaps. Ensure that you maintain a low burn rate (editor's note: don't burn too much money); keep your job in the meantime, so you don't come under pressure from personal financial difficulties. You and your business will have time to prepare for the next successful startup. When I started LanguageWire, I worked as a waiter and bartender at night to be able to afford to work during the day on my startup, which didn't pay any salary for the first year.

Everything starts small (and by chance)

Do yourself a favor: when you hear about successful startups such as Facebook, GoMore, and Airbnb, find out what their first 3 years were like. They all started quite small and by chance, and no one could predict how large they would become in reality. They started small, tasted the market, had a long product–market fit phase before they hit the bull's-eye with the concept, and *bang!* they were on their way.

Exercise patience, maintain a low burn rate, find five customers, get a perfect product–market fit, and fly…

Good luck!

—

I LIKE TO BEGIN WHERE WINDS SHAKE THE FIRST BRANCH.

Odysseus Elytis

MURRAY NEWLANDS
Learning to become an entrepreneur

Murray Newlands (United Kingdom) is an entrepreneur, investor, business advisor, and speaker. He has founded a number of interesting startups and has been named as one of the 50 most influential marketers in the world by *Entrepreneur* magazine.

Murray Newlands lives in the United States but is originally from the United Kingdom. He gained his green card by being recognized by the US government as an "alien of extraordinary ability," and that alone made me interested in understanding how this very successful entrepreneur and speaker thinks and acts.

How has Murray Newlands managed to become such a good entrepreneur, and how do you go from being a lawyer in a well-paid but pretty ordinary job to being recognized by *Entrepreneur* magazine as one of the top 50 most influential marketers in the world?

In *The GuruBook*, you can read about impressive startups turning into billion-dollar companies, but let us be honest: Most startups actually fail. Is there a way to learn to become an entrepreneur?

When you startup a business, statistically it's very unlikely to work. Just look at how venture capitalists view their investments. They know that if they're lucky, 1 out of 10 of their investments will become a big success. So it's in the DNA of ambitious startups that not all of them are going to work out.

I think a lot of people are attracted to entrepreneurship because they don't like their job. However, starting up a company is not a quick way to have a more interesting everyday life. It can indeed be very stressful in the beginning. Lots of worries, lots of failures, and so on.

That is why I suggest training to become an entrepreneur rather than creating an ambitious tech startup from day one.

How do you train to become an entrepreneur?

When I started my first company, I had very little money and experience. My business was a consultancy firm, so I was selling my time. That meant that I didn't need a lot of capital investment, and if it failed, it would not be the end of the world for me.

When we talk about training to become an entrepreneur you can actually do that from a very early age. Kids do it all the time without thinking that they're learning how to build companies. A kid might open a sweet stand and realize that it's both fun and brings in a little money. Then this kid might open two more sweet stands, and now he or she is turning into an actual entrepreneur. In this process, the kid will make a lot of mistakes, but when you still live with your parents, you don't have to worry about not being able to pay your rent. The same is the case if you start up a small business, while you're still studying.

But what if the job that you're able to create, while you're still studying, is not your dream job?

It probably isn't. That is why I talk about learning to become an entrepreneur. With your first company you might know that it will not deliver everything that you want. But it's an investment in learning how to start up businesses.

Imagine that my dream is to build a sharing economy app within the industry of cleaning buildings and private homes. Should I then start by doing the actual cleaning in these homes?

Yes, that is a great idea, because through this experience you will understand much more about the customers' needs, their pains, worries, and so on. You get to know your target audience, so you're much better equipped at the next big step of trying to digitalize some of this industry.

In fact, I've written an article with 75 ideas for businesses you can launch for cheap or free. This is also a signal that entrepreneurship doesn't have to start with trying to build the next Uber or Amazon. Oftentimes, it's best not to aim that high the first time.

Today, many people are looking to leave the daily grind for something that feeds their passion. People do not want to retire at the age of 60 only to look back on life and feel they have wasted it. Luckily, it is now increasingly easy to start a business from scratch without spending a fortune.

In the article that I mentioned, I've highlighted 75 varied business ideas you can start cheaply from the comfort of your own home. Some of the business ideas require nothing more than an internet connection.

Can you give a few examples?

If you're great with numbers, you could become a freelance bookkeeper, because you do not need to be a certified public accountant. There are lots of free-to-use online invoicing tools such as Sighted.com and online payment tools like Due.com. Some services you could offer include creating balance sheets, providing income statements, and creating various monthly, quarterly, or annual financial reports.

Another example could be offering remote secretarial services. All you need is strong organizational skills, good communication skills, good time management, and a high level of autonomy.

Your day-to-day tasks as a freelancing secretary would then typically include booking meetings, organizing calendars, replying to emails, putting together presentations, and answering phone calls.

A third and increasingly popular opportunity is becoming a YouTuber, blogger, or vlogger. If you're an expert in a specific field—for instance, travel, fashion, cooking, and so on—or if you know how to do something particularly well, why not tell the world through a blog or vlog? All you will need is a computer and a good-quality camera. You can make money by offering advertising space and reviews of products on your platform.

This also answers my question about whether getting funding is critical for every entrepreneur.

That always depends. If you can launch a company and grow without funding, of course that leaves you with the entire ownership of your business. That is good both in the many situations where you don't actually need funding, but it can also be an idea if you choose to grow organically and bootstrap your business.

However, there are also many startup ideas that need lots of capital to grow and succeed. In these cases, remember not to lose focus on making your business and products great. Getting an investment in your business is a very time-consuming thing, and you see a lot of startups forgetting about building their business when they're out there searching for money. That is very dangerous.

What is your best advice on how to get funding?

If you decide that your business is ready for funding, then read about how to find and pitch to investors. Build a great story around your product and remember that investors hate product details and features. They fall in love with a combination of story, numbers, and you.

If you approach rich families or individuals that invest in startups, they often don't just focus on the return but also want to help out within sectors such as education, environment, and so on. So if your business is within one of these sectors, it could be a good idea to approach these kinds of private investors before going to the more professional business angels and venture capitalists.

You have to think of investment as selling something. Study how to make that sales pitch. Have the right material in hand. If someone walked up to you in the street with a great idea and wanted a million dollars, you wouldn't give it to them. This is also why one of the best ways to get investment is to be referred to the person by

someone. Before you want funding, get to know people within the investment opportunity. Make sure that they know about you and your project in advance. That will hugely increase your odds of success.

How do you build such an investor network?

Lots of entrepreneurs call or email potential investors out of the blue. They very rarely succeed, because these investors get so many requests and almost automatically turn away people that they don't know or have never heard about.

It's really important to get to know these people face-to-face. Go to events within your niche and network with investors. Ask good questions such as, What are you looking to invest in?

Remember that if they're not interested in your particular area, they can still be a very important connection for you. You can help them out by finding other startups that match their criteria, and if you start doing so, you'll find out that they will also connect you with relevant investors from their own network.

Referrals is the most important thing in investing. I've interviewed a lot of venture capitalists, and they say that they don't invest in a company unless it is referred to them. Sometimes there is an exception, but around 95% of their investments come from referrals.

As Robert Foster Bennett once said, "In sales, a referral is key to the door of resistance."

Exactly.

WHEN YOU CEASE TO DREAM, YOU CEASE TO LIVE.

Malcolm Forbes

CHRISTIAN LANNG
Leadership from the trenches

Christian Lanng (Denmark) is CEO, co-founder, and board member of Tradeshift, the largest platform of its sort in the world. Lanng is a member of the Global Agenda Council of the future of IT software and services, World Economic Forum.

Ben Horowitz recently published his book *The Hard Things about Hard Things*. It's no exaggeration to say I love it. As a third-time founder having experienced many of the challenges firsthand, I wish that book had been written 15 years ago, when I was trying to build my first company (although I'm not sure I would have read it back then; learning seems to be easier in hindsight). One of the great things about Ben's book is that it focuses on sharing the hard lessons, when it's not all smooth sailing.

Inspired by this, I thought I would add some of the lessons from Tradeshift. Just like Opsware, Tradeshift is a company in wartime, as are most B2B companies trying to break into highly entrenched software markets controlled by incumbents with massive cash moats. At Tradeshift, we have been fairly lucky in our ability to attract high-level investors who believe in our vision and who want to back us for the long term, but that doesn't mean every single day isn't a fight.

The topic I want to focus on is leadership. Three years ago at a dinner with Ben White and Stephen Chandler from Notion Capital, I asked them what had been the hardest part of scaling their company, Message Labs,

from a startup to a US$750 million exit. They both replied without blinking: scaling leadership above 100 people.

Curious, and still full of youthful arrogance, I asked why. "Isn't it just a matter of hiring the right people?"

Stephen patiently explained to me it was not as simple as that. You need to build a culture, training, and leaders, and make sure communication is aligned all the way through the company. You can't rely on your own ability as a founder to just stand on a soapbox and be heard and understood.

Talking to other CEOs and co-founders, it's clear to me that lack of clear leadership across the organization is what kills most C- or later-stage companies. Having talked earlier about how we handled culture and leadership in the earlier stages of Tradeshift's history, I thought I would share how we organize leadership at Tradeshift today and some my own beliefs about what makes for efficient leaders.

A few months ago, we had a Global Leader Camp, which is our own new talent and leadership development program at Tradeshift. We invited 27 current managers or people who were seen as leaders in the company from their actions or roles, making sure to both include current leaders and the talent for the next generation of leaders.

The goal was to make this a generation of leaders that would help shape Tradeshift through the next 3 years and lead from the front line. We focused on leadership and not so much management (leadership is the job of setting direction and inspiring others, management is the process of getting shit done), as we already have a very strong results culture. We wanted to make everyone capable leaders of product, people, and vision in the diverse and challenging environment that is Tradeshift.

One of the reasons we started this program was to get away from relying solely on the *founder signal*—where leadership was basically me or my co-founders getting up on that soapbox and having everyone listen and be inspired. We needed leadership on the ground. We were seeing too many people feeling disconnected from the vision of Tradeshift and what it meant for them, too much cynicism (building highly complex B2B products in wartime will do that to you), and people who loved Tradeshift but were starting to burn out after 3 years of running at maximum speed. You can't just wish these issues away or do an even more powerful speech to have them disappear. As a founder or CEO, you need to go to the root cause and, even more scarily, hand over some responsibility to others in maintaining and building the vision.

As a leader, you have to realize that the only real tool you have is yourself, your own experiences, your beliefs, and your ability to execute. It's an extremely exposed position, because any failure points to flaws in what makes you who you are. It's also extremely rewarding to succeed, as you are growing personally.

So the first disclaimer is that what works for me might not work for you, and that's ok—as long as you do believe something and use that in the way you lead others. I encourage everyone to find out what works for him or her.

So, adding a little bit of context on my core beliefs:

Startups are factories of make-believe.

Everyone remember that scene from Peter Pan where he tells you that you can fly if you just believe it? Stepping out of that window and trusting this radical move is the same thing as working for a startup. A startup is only suspended by the collective belief of the people who work to build it, its investors, and its customers.

That also means you must always walk that fine line between hope and cheerleading and being realistic and critical. You can challenge the direction in which you are flying but never whether it's possible to fly (unless you want to crash badly). At Tradeshift, we typically say it's great to be critical but sucks to be cynical (permanently not believing in anything).

Flying requires bold and visionary ambition.

This next step is almost as important as believing you can fly. Make sure you have a bold and visionary ambition. People generally won't risk their life (or time) on something that is not meaningful. Very few people will take that step into emptiness to make 1%-better toilet paper. This goes for both your company and your team. Make sure the goals you set and the team is connected to the vision of the company and not just "make it 1% better."

Vision without execution is just hallucination.

It feels really nice but doesn't do shit. When you are challenging people to trust you, to take the leap into emptiness, it's really easy to get called a liar if you fail. The only difference between being a liar or a visionary is execution. Once you have taken the jump, work your butt off to make sure that the vision becomes reality. You need to cross that chasm of disbelief and the only way to do it is by proving it through execution.

Lead from the front.

In the second year of Tradeshift, I was sitting together with a new colleague getting our board presentation ready for the next day at 1:00 a.m. I felt really sorry that he had to spend his night like this, and I told him that I was really sorry. He looked at me and said, "That's no problem, and the difference between tonight and my old job is that my CEO would never had been sitting next to me."

There are plenty of long nights, weeks, months, years in any startup; remember that everyone is watching you, and if you are the first to shovel shit, they will follow.

Fight for your vision, always.

Quitting is for pussies. This is Ben Horowitz's advice for CEOs, but I think it's valid advice for any leader pursuing an idea. Any new idea that matters meets massive resistance, so get ready to fight for it. The difference between a leader and everyone else is often how much they are willing to fight for their ideas.

Challenge conventional wisdom.

Ben Horowitz talks about *selection bias*, which is what happens when decisions are close to 50/50 and leaders go with the group because they are afraid of being alone when they fail (better to fail as a team). This is not just something that matters between a CEO and his board but all the way down in an organization. Leaders are leaders because they dare to make controversial decisions and stick to them, even when they go against the grain of the group.

Be the first to change direction when needed.

You have to fight for your vision and challenge the conventional wisdom. But you also need to be the first to change direction if your decision was wrong. Don't cling to it because you are afraid of losing face. The ability to let go and move on is one of the most important skills of a leader.

Practice radical trust.

If somebody fucks up, the biggest thing you can do is help him or her, rather than blaming or yelling. Trust me, they will remember that a hundred times more than you being angry. In Tradeshift, we practice radical trust in the people we hire and give them a lot of freedom, and when they screw up, we don't take it away. We encourage them to move on and learn.

Vulnerability is a strength, not a weakness.

I'm an insecure overachiever and I can be afraid that others will think that the incredibly skilled and experienced leaders working for me are better than me. But I'm not afraid of showing that vulnerability. Through the years, I have learned it's better to be real and flawed as a leader rather than trying to project a picture of constant perfection. Everyone will have an easier time relating to you, and they will not abandon you the moment you fail (and you will fail many times).

These are the beliefs that have helped me navigate as a leader and what I shared with the next generation of leaders in Tradeshift. Together with an intense program of strength-based leadership training, coaching, cultural leadership, and working with real-life leadership challenges, I'm sure we have created a strong generation of leaders in Tradeshift who will help lead from the trenches for the next 3 years.

LARS FJELDSØE-NIELSEN
"B2Both": Why all startup founders need a growth currency

Lars Fjeldsøe-Nielsen (Denmark) joined Balderton Capital in 2015 after roles at three of Silicon Valley's best-known tech companies: Uber, WhatsApp, and Dropbox. As head of mobile at Dropbox, where he was one of the firm's first 25 employees, his distribution deal-making helped the file-sharing company reach its first 100 million users.

It was 2011, and as I stood up in the conference room at Dropbox's San Francisco headquarters, I knew that the pitch I was about to deliver would quite possibly make me the least popular person in the building. As (then) head of mobile at the fast-growing file-sharing and storage startup, the strategy I was poised to outline would involve redrawing the company roadmap and the inevitable jettisoning of long-planned projects, which some in the room that day—who included the engineering leadership teams, alongside the founder and CEO Drew Houston—had sweated blood over.

My plan, inspired by Dropbox's pioneering *freemium* business growth model, which way back in 2008 offered users 2 GB of free storage and 50 GB for $9.99 a month or $99.99 a year, was to strike a partnership deal with Samsung in which our technology would come embedded on the Korean manufacturer's latest handsets. When owners unwrapped their new device and powered up, the first screen they'd see would offer them 50 GB of free storage for 2 years—enough to back up (approximately) 27,000 photos.

To validate this strategy, we had built a growth projection, based on the way we modeled new feature and product launches, which demonstrated that if Samsung shipped us on 200 million handsets, and a sizeable portion of those new owners signed up to Dropbox as a result, the upheaval caused internally would be more than justified.

The year 2012—when the groundbreaking iPhone 5 appeared—was a tipping point for mobile, particularly in the United States, where smartphone penetration grew to 55.5% of the population, from just 41% a year earlier, according to Nielsen. Meanwhile, Facebook's monthly active users on mobile grew almost 10 times, from 58 million in Q4 2011 to 526 million just 3 years later. So it was against this transition-to-mobile backdrop that Drew green lit the Samsung partnership (and one with HTC too). The impact was both instant and game-changing. In the summer of 2012, as *Forbes* reported, the majority of Dropbox sign-ups were mobile users for the first time, due to a combination of our partnerships and the general trends toward mobile. Ultimately, it led us to over 100 million registered users and was the foundation for a patent we filed on it.

Personally, it represented a Eureka moment. I came to describe this strategy as devising a *growth currency*, where something of genuine value, be it free storage space or a code or voucher to share with friends, can be traded or offered to turbocharge viral growth. While a startup needs to have genuine growth to begin with—this is no quick fix or cure-all for a failing product—the keys to launching a successful growth currency are timing and value. As a founder, you need to surface your growth currency at a moment of high intent, such as when a customer has just removed their new handset from its box and is in the frame of mind to spend half an hour or so willingly setting up their new toy and trying out new services.

Catch them with an attractive offer at that point and the likelihood is high they will sign up. What's more, you also have a rare and fleeting opportunity to "educate" users about your product's features at the very moment their tolerance threshold for experimenting with a new service is at its highest. For Dropbox that meant, among other things, being able to show new users how to sync between devices and letting them know they can share files with others.

The second thing to bear in mind about growth currencies is that they should always be data inspired, rather than based on (albeit educated) guesswork or, worse, a hunch. With Dropbox, we knew exactly how much free storage space to offer, because our decision-making was based on data from existing user behavior. Giving away 50 GB wouldn't cost us much more than, say, 30 GB, and we knew the "wow factor" perception of offering so much storage space would create consumer buzz.

At Uber, meanwhile—where I was VP mobile— we used (and they still use) a different type of growth currency—namely, a promotional code that can be shared with a friend who's new to Uber, so that you both receive a financial credit toward future rides (the precise monetary value of this promotion has fluctuated, depending on when and where it was offered.) Although the acquisition cost of each customer is high in this case, it results in explosive sign-up rates for new riders, the vast majority of whom go on to become repeat users, and in turn refer other new users.

Uber has deployed a wide variety of spins on this particular growth currency. When I was there, we also experimented with sending notifications to existing users around certain events or locations, where once again intent was high. For Valentine's, for example, we messaged riders with a time-limited code which unlocked a free trip or upgrade for use that night. We offered a similar and hugely successful promotion around certain airports: when people switched on their phones at JFK in New York, they could redeem a free ride into the city.

A US-wide promotion in June 2016, meanwhile, saw Uber team up with Sprint to offer passengers 50% off their journey to watch Copa América Centenario matches—a great way, in this instance, to gain traction within America's soccer-loving Latino population. Partnerships such as these are a way to further accelerate growth, through leveraging a heavyweight partner (Samsung, for example, spent an estimated $14 billion on marketing and advertising globally in 2013) and are often a critical element in a growth currency's effectiveness.

In 2014, I helped Uber forge just such a partnership with Carlos Slim's América Móvil, the telecoms giant. Over a full day's meeting with Carlos, his sons, and other top executives at his offices in Mexico City, we struck a deal in which millions of América Móvil customers would be offered a discount on their first Uber ride. The business case made perfect sense for the carrier, who was able to offer something extra of value to its users, while it was a way for us to fuel growth in Latin America (having already proven the model in the United States by teaming up with AT&T).

In fact, so successful is this strategy that I've long urged every startup I work with—as an advisor or, today, an investor—to identify a growth currency as soon as they have significant customer traction. At Pocket, whom I advised in 2015, this led the team to build a premium product with additional functionality—something a certain tranche of users would pay for—before striking a partnership deal with Mozilla, where Pocket would be integrated into Mozilla's browser. (The deal was agreed quickly, as Mozilla were launching a new version of their browser, which they wanted Pocket to be part of.) Once again, it was a win–win arrangement: Pocket had access to Mozilla's hundreds of millions of users globally, who would in turn get a free subscription to Pocket's premium service. Ultimately, of course, the synergy was so compelling that Mozilla acquired Pocket.

Indeed, whether it's Evernote embedding their services into NTT DoCoMo, Japan's leading mobile operator, WhatsApp's estimated 100-plus operator deals globally (in which I played the role of fixer), Spotify's multiple partnerships, which include an ongoing deal with Vodafone (which currently offers Vodafone customers a free 24-month subscription to Spotify Premium when they buy a pay-monthly entertainment plan), or Netflix's deals with, among others, Comcast, Liberty Global, and leading Indian carriers, wherever you look, the majority of the major internet and mobile brands have growth currencies in place to power growth. Three of the largest public technology companies in the United States—Microsoft (partnerships with Dell and Workday), Apple (premium print products), and Amazon (Prime and Pantry)—use similar tactics, albeit in a range of different guises.

If the first question growth founders should ask themselves is "What's my growth currency?", the next is "Where on the spectrum between prioritizing user numbers and revenues do I want to be?"

Of the former category, Facebook, WhatsApp, and Snapchat are prime examples of an approach best summed up as "If you build global scale, then revenues will follow." The second approach is to grow a significant paying customer base, either through subscribers (Netflix) or a highly monetized model (Uber) or through a freemium model (LinkedIn, Spotify, or Dropbox). On the whole—although this is no immutable law—the user-driven end of the spectrum tends to be populated with B2C companies and the "dollar" end with B2B.

Now, in my experience, there is a midway point on the spectrum; a sweet spot where companies are able to appeal both to individuals and enterprises simultaneously. A case in point is Spotify, which recently hit the 60 million paying subscribers milestone and has now launched Soundtrack Your Brand, an enterprise-facing spin-off and a recent Balderton investment. Another example is Google, whose Gmail service and apps such as Drive, Calendar, Sheets, and Docs, are perfectly positioned to appeal to consumers as well as paying business subscribers.

I call this sweet spot on the user numbers–dollar spectrum *B2Both*. Businesses who can capture both these markets (i.e., consumer and enterprise) simultaneously invariably experience surging growth. So the third and final question founders should ask themselves is this: "Is there a way for my product or service to operate as a B2Both company?" Move into that space where you're woven seamlessly into people's personal and work lives, and the chances are you've found growth's answer to the Holy Grail. Indeed, so convinced am I of this sweet spot that I predict even that titan of B2C corporations, Facebook, will over time pivot to B2Both, perhaps by acquiring Slack as a catapult. Only then can it truly claim to have succeeded in its mission to "make the world more open and connected."

One company that has already made this shift is Dropbox, however, which saw its popularity among consumers at home gradually carried across into the workplace, so that today it can reasonably be described as a B2Both company. I won't claim that this is something I predicted when I made the case for partnering up with Samsung all those years ago. But two things have become abundantly clear to me since. First, the fast lane to growth begins with a growth currency. And second, without one, the road ahead narrows by the day.

ERIK ANDERSON
Catching waves

Erik Anderson (United States) is one of the world's top global innovation leaders, investors, and philanthropists. He is founder and CEO of WestRiver Group, which provides integrated capital solutions for the global innovation economy. He has also been named one of the 100 Most Intriguing Entrepreneurs of 2017 by Goldman Sachs.

Erik Anderson is a world leader, entrepreneur, and investor by heart. He currently works as co-chairman and CEO of Topgolf Entertainment Group, a global sports entertainment company. In this role, he has received numerous honors, including the 2014 Ernst & Young Entrepreneur of the Year Award in the Southwest region.

Erik is also on the board of directors for Singularity University, a global community using exponential technologies to tackle the world's biggest challenges.

I (Jonathan) sat down with Erik to talk about startups, building companies, and how to catch waves.

Please share the story about your latest golf startup with me.

Topgolf originated back in 2000 in the United Kingdom with two brothers who invented a way to track golf balls using radio frequency identification (RFID) sensors. They started Topgolf by enhancing a driving range with this technology and opened three locations around the London area, all of which are still operating today. In 2005, I was part of a group of investors that brought the concept to the United States, starting with Alexandria,

Chicago, and Dallas. We spent several years improving the design and perfecting the model—adding to the menu, enlarging the venues, creating programming and events, and so on. The venue went from 60 bays to 102, with 500 associates and a full kitchen and sports bar.

TOP originally stood for *target-oriented practice*. That's probably the best way to compare where we started versus where we are now. If you think about our current customer base, it's a good thing we called it Topgolf, because no one would go to Target-Oriented Practice Golf. Now, you go to Topgolf for parties and events and nightlife. So that probably captures the two ends of the spectrum. We started to become an experience.

When did you get actively involved in the company?

I started as CEO and chairman in 2012 with my partners Neil, Randy, and Richard Grogan, and we really focused on the experience element. That led to the next level of growth. Along the way, we started to observe how large our audience was; we were getting half a million visits per site. I was thinking about what to do with that audience and by analogy observed Major League Baseball's MLBAM and Red Bull Media. It became evident that that could be a good model and decided it was the smart thing to do. We started to look for how would we do it, and we found a company called World Golf Tour. They were the largest digital golf audience and had a good team and creative capabilities, so we thought they could form the basis of Topgolf Media. Lucky for us, they were available for sale. We got into the process late, but we moved quickly and acquired them.

We also acquired Protracer, which was another great technology company, and all of that has converged now into what Topgolf is today. There are a lot of moving parts, but the most important lesson was adapting to the experiential economy and the emerging millennial consumer. We caught that wave.

How important is it to draw up a business plan and market analysis? Is it a waste of time and "old school," or what do you think?

It's great to aggregate information and it's great to understand markets. It's absolutely important to do the analysis because it informs your thinking. But it's also important that you have the willingness to look at your own best thinking and say, I think the value proposition can overcome the data.

If you had done a market analysis on Topgolf at the time, what would have been the result?

I actually think that the analysis would have told us not to do it. There had been many driving range ideas: Jack Nicklaus tried one; other people took a run at building nicer facilities and family golf centers, and those sorts of things had failed. So, the analysis would have challenged us.

The question is, Are you going to be controlled by the past? We looked at the market, but then we said to ourselves, This is a digital, interactive game; maybe the technology changes it. Maybe it's a different group of consumers. Although you had to be really smart to see that millennials were going to turn out to be experiential consumers. What makes everything look so good in retrospect is that it seems like we saw something others didn't. We didn't necessarily see it 10 years ago, but like I said earlier, we were able to adapt and catch the wave. The market analysis is naturally going to be constrained by available data and best practices, and it might not reflect your best thinking. That is the point of departure as to whether you go forward or not.

Should you do a business plan?

Yes, but realize that everyone overestimates their understanding. Some people might think it's a waste of time because doing a plan assumes that you know a lot of things and that it will be a linear journey. You will notice most business plans are very linear. It's an excellent discipline, but realize that if you have a large value proposition and you have a plan to get there, the probability that the original plan will get you there is low. It's new, so by definition, you can only understand so much of it.

In your opinion, why do most startups fail?

Most startups fail because it's hard. There are so many things that have to go right, so there's a lot of luck. People might go back and try to find patterns and say it's always A, B, or C. Someone said that startups fail because they run out of money. If someone keeps giving you money, you'll never fail, or at least you'll keep going. But I think it's just hard.

Deeper below that, there is a point that's consistent with the question about investors. An important practice for us is making the distinction between volatility, learning, and mistakes. Many things can be misinterpreted as strong signals that cause you to quit or lose confidence in management, when in reality it was (1) you had an understanding gap or (2) there was volatility.

If we look at Topgolf, there could have been all sorts of places where we missed a number or we were behind, and you could have interpreted that as poor management or a bad model, but really it was just volatility. Luckily, we had the right investors, so we could have an informed conversation about what was happening. It wasn't always a strict assessment of where management failed. Sometimes it's just learning. People often confuse a learning moment with a failure moment.

As an investor, how do you know if you are investing in the right company or not? What parameters do you look at?

I always look for something that has a significant value proposition. It sounds simple, but sometimes you have to dig hard to see where it is. Docusign was a classic example. When we looked at Docusign as an investor in the Series B, which was an early round, the value proposition was simple. We could charge $0.40 to get something signed, accurately and on time. It was also greener and much faster. People were spending $30 sending signatures back and forth on FedEx. A significant portion of FedEx's revenue at the time was packages for signatures. And that's assuming you got it right the first time. If you could solve that problem and take just 10% from FedEx,

then that was a really good business. The big question there was whether it would be an enforceable signature.

What about the investment in Topgolf?

Topgolf was simple. A driving range bay typically had one person in it and they hit a bucket of balls for maybe $10. We put four to six people in it and added beer and food. The simple math said if they spent twice as much and you put four people in the bay, you were getting eight times the revenue per unit. There was a very clear model and value proposition. So, I tried to unbundle all the pieces of the model, whether it was the margin on food or the staffing model or the technology, and see if there was an example anywhere in the market for each element. Then all I was doing was aggregating existing elements that are operating that way at scale, so I know it's doable, I can find people and systems to do it, and I know I will have flow-through to the bottom line.

Typically, not all the elements of the model are new. Many of them are being used in other businesses. If I can unbundle them and have reference points and I can understand the buildup to the value proposition, then I know over time I will be able to get there.

How important is culture and purpose?

Culture and purpose are more important than ever, for both the employee and customer. Having a higher purpose—in Topgolf's case it's "connecting people in meaningful ways"—creates a powerful culture within the company. This culture is what drives the employees of today—they are motivated not by money, but by creating amazing experiences for our guests, by building bonds with their coworkers, and by seeing the good we can do in the community. The modern customer is similar. With unlimited options available, people are drawn to brands that are authentic and purposeful. Simon Sinek talks about this in his book *Start With Why*. People don't buy what you do, but why you do it. If our guests can see that Topgolf really does connect people in meaningful ways and does good in our communities, they are more likely to come back to connect with us and feel good about doing so.

METTE LYKKE
Entrepreneurship is a marathon, not a sprint

Mette Lykke is co-founder of Endomondo—a social fitness network with more than 30 million users—acquired by athletic apparel maker Under Armour for $85 million in 2015. She currently works as CEO of Too Good To Go—the World's largest consumer platform for surplus food.

When entrepreneurs are successful, we are enormously interested in what made them become entrepreneurs. It's as if their main achievement is the decision to say goodbye to the secure and safe life—the sure job, the safe pay, and the good CV. While the choice of taking the plunge is definitely a precondition for success, it is quite far from being the primary achievement. The difficult part is not becoming an entrepreneur but remaining one when things look hopeless and everyone around you has lost faith.

We love stories about how two 15-year-old kids in a basement have a good idea, get a breakthrough on the first day, and become a global success a year later. In reality, however, building a business and generating real value takes time. It is in no way abnormal for a startup to use 5–10 years to make a serious breakthrough. Along the way, you will undoubtedly experience a lot of adversity, and sometimes, the hard times will turn into negative spirals that it takes time to come out of again.

As an entrepreneur, I've had my fair share of these periods, and based on my experience, I have listed seven pieces of advice for other entrepreneurs, which I hope can give them inspiration to move ahead.

1. Believe in your concept, your team, and yourself.

"But there's no GPS in mobile phones." "Who in their right mind would run around with their mobile phone?" We heard those two objections time and again when we established Endomondo. There will always be people who don't believe in your idea and who are not afraid to tell you so. Console yourself with the thought that if your idea was so obvious that everyone understood it, then someone would have launched it already. If the idea feels right to you, then it doesn't really matter whether other people believe in it or not. As long as you believe in it, in your team, and not least in yourself, it has a chance of being successful in the end. Get energy from the rejections—and look forward to the day when the doubters must eat their own words.

2. Remind yourself and the team why you're here.

There will be days when only your passion for the concept and the product will keep you and the team going. You should always remember what a difference your product makes and why your vision is worth fighting for—and vocalize it again and again. Hang the vision, the mission, and the values up on the office walls, so everyone is reminded about them every day. And if they haven't been written down, have a teambuilding day with the whole team, so you can define them once and for all, and where everyone can take ownership of them. Involve your customers as well; ask for feedback on the product and share success stories with the team. Every day we receive hundreds of emails from our users at Endomondo, and some of them go straight to the heart. When a user has lost 70 kilos by using our app and is now able to play with his children again, it's hard not to feel that our product is worth fighting for.

3. Hire only people who share your vision.

Simon Sinek, who also contributes to this book, had this piece of advice in his fantastic TED Talk, and it really is something important to comply with. Nobody is successful in business without the backing of a team of really good people; entrepreneurship is a team sport. In adversity, in particular, you need a team that is focused, and if your employees don't believe in the vision and the difference you can make, motivating them becomes much more difficult. So, avoid applicants who only want a job and a paycheck at the end of the month; they can find that elsewhere.

4. Focus on the positive news.

In times of adversity, the ratio of good to bad news is very unequal. You'll get perhaps 10 bad news reports for every good news report, and holding on to the positive aspects is very important for morale. Share the positive stories internally, so the whole team can get a boost every time something goes well. Have a little celebration when something succeeds; it doesn't have to be a large, expensive party every time. Consider also not talking solely about the challenges at your meetings. At our management meetings, we decided that every participant had to start by talking about the three most positive developments since the last meeting. Only then would we discuss the challenges.

It's also important to be positive away from the job. Inspired by these meetings, my husband and I introduced the same idea at home; we would mention the three most positive things from the past day during dinner. In fact, it's a very sound habit that can be recommended generally.

5. Be present at the office.

When your startup has problems, you as leader must fight alongside your team. This means that you must be present physically and mentally, and that you don't succumb to the temptation to accept invitations to meetings and speeches around the world unless those arrangements really benefit your business. Minimize your traveling to the absolutely necessary and help keep the team's spirit high.

6. Sleep on it.

Entrepreneurship is a marathon, not a sprint. Unlike a traditional marathon, you don't know the distance from the start, and that makes distributing your energy correctly along the way vital. If you start off by working all the time and not getting enough sleep, there's a significant risk that you'll run out of steam within a year or two. There's a reason why deprivation of sleep is a well-known torture instrument. If you don't get sufficient sleep over a long period, you become less efficient, and the negative spiral really takes off when you try to compensate for the lack of efficiency by working even more and sleeping even less. Sooner or later, you will at best lose the big picture and at worst you will burn out; both can be fatal for your business. Prioritize to let your body and mind have the peace to charge for a new and efficient day.

7. Have something else in your life.

During the first years as an entrepreneur, I was so fired up that I was never pleased with our results or able to take things easy. I was always en route toward the next milestone and the next target. It wasn't until I had a baby that I learned to love the journey we were on—at least sometimes. Having something else and more important in my life has helped me put the professional challenges into perspective. When things go badly with the business, coming home to a little one, who's mostly interested in whether you're singing children's songs correctly and remember all the verses, is totally therapeutic.

Generally, a difficult aspect in adverse times is being uncertain of when developments will turn positive again. "One day at a time" is the only theorem that works, and so it is a paradox that it requires just as much patience as impatience. Every day the impatience contributes to the plans being executed, but at the same time, a certain degree of patience is necessary since coming out on top can easily take many months. On the other hand, it feels so fantastic when you're on top of things again that it's worth the wait and the hard work.

I'VE LEARNED THAT FINISHING
A MARATHON ISN'T JUST AN
ATHLETIC ACHIEVEMENT. IT'S
A STATE OF MIND; A STATE OF
MIND THAT SAYS ANYTHING
IS POSSIBLE.

John Hanc

BRIAN CHESKY
How to build culture

Brian Chesky (United States) is an internet entrepreneur who co-founded the hospitality exchange service Airbnb. Chesky is the CEO of the company and was named one of *Time*'s 100 Most Influential People of 2015.

I sent the following letter to our entire team at Airbnb.

Hey team,

Our next team meeting is dedicated to Core Values, which are essential to building our culture. It occurred to me that before this meeting, I should write you a short letter on why culture is so important to Joe, Nate, and me.

After we closed our Series C with Peter Thiel in 2012, we invited him to our office. This was late last year, and we were in the Berlin room showing him various metrics. Midway through the conversation, I asked him what was the single most important piece of advice he had for us.

He replied, "Don't fuck up the culture."

This wasn't what we were expecting from someone who just gave us $150 million. I asked him to elaborate on this. He said one of the reasons he invested in us was our culture. But he had a somewhat cynical view that it was practically inevitable, once a company gets to a certain size, to "fuck it up." Hmm. How depressing, I thought.

Were we destined to eventually "fuck up our culture"? We talked about it a bit more, and it became clear that it was possible to defend, and actually build, the culture. But it had to be one of the things we were most focused on. I thought to myself, How many company CEOs are focused on culture above all else? Is it the metric they measure closest? Is it what they spend most of their hours on each week?

Culture is simply a shared way of doing something with passion.

Our culture is the foundation for our company. We may not be remembered for much after we are gone, and if Airbnb is around 100 years from now, surely we won't be a booking website for homes. We will be far past this in our evolution (not to mention that kids 100 years from now will be asking their grandparents what websites were).

The thing that will endure for 100 years, the way it has for most 100-year companies, is the culture. The culture is what creates the foundation for all future innovation. If you break the culture, you break the machine that creates your products.

So how do we build culture?

By upholding our core values in everything we do. Culture is a thousand things, a thousand times. It's living the core values when you hire, when you write an email, when you are working on a project, when you are walking in the hall. We have the power, by living the values, to build the culture. We also have the power, by breaking the values, to fuck up the culture. Each one of us has this opportunity, this burden.

Why is culture so important to a business? Here is a simple way to frame it: The stronger the culture, the less corporate process a company needs. When the culture is strong, you can trust everyone to do the right thing. People can be independent and autonomous. They can be entrepreneurial. And if we have a company that is entrepreneurial in spirit, we will be able to take our next "(wo)man on the moon" leap. Ever notice how families or tribes don't require much process? That is because there is such a strong trust and culture that it supersedes any process. In organizations (or even in a society) where culture is weak, you need an abundance of heavy, precise rules and processes.

There are days when it's easy to feel the pressure of our own growth expectations, other days when we need to ship product. Others still where we are dealing with the latest government relations issue. It's easy to get consumed by these. And they are all very important. But compared to culture, they are relatively short term. These problems will come and go. But culture is forever.

Brian

Note to readers: Previously published on Brian's personal blog.

TINE THYGESEN
Why culture is just as important for tech startups as tech

Tine Thygesen (Denmark) is CEO of Mesh, Founders House, and Startup Village, and is on a mission to build superior physical locations and networks to empower creators, entrepreneurs, and change-makers. She has started and led five companies and has been named among the Top 10 Speakers on Tech in Europe.

When a well-known brand like IBM or Nike are recruiting new people, they don't only have the advantage of the brand but also of high salaries and good perks. An employee signing up at Microsoft essentially gets paid while learning and building up a good CV. And if she would want to leave later, she is well positioned.

As a startup, you have to compete with this, with no initial brand, no impressive salaries, and no perks. Therefore, you need to deliver something else. What you can deliver is a superior culture.

Culture is one aspect where it should be easy for startups to compete with big corporations. Because startups are small and young, they can be innovative, flexible, fast moving, and fun. They can be more grounded in their values and be better at selecting people with the same worldview. A place where you smile when you go to work in the morning because you know you'll go home smarter is startup culture at its best.

There are three cornerstones to building a great startup culture:

1. The founders and execs must see themselves as "first among equals."

2. Delegate responsibility, not just tasks.

3. Provide a clear mission.

Being first among equals sums up the core of modern leadership. While founders, executives, and CEOs play a unique role in the company, we're not more important than anyone else. Because a company is an engine of interdependent functions, it is no stronger than its weakest link. That makes everyone important. It takes humility to appreciate this, and humility isn't always the strong trait in entrepreneurs. It is, however, a leadership trait that creates huge loyalty.

Twice in my career, I have worked in companies where someone in a leading role has lacked humility. Both times, it led to poor culture, low commitment, and high employee churn.

The second area where startups can outcompete corporations is in terms of delegating responsibility. Many people feel unheard and underutilized in their current jobs, and they seek out startups because of the opportunity to play a larger role and have more influence. This is a perfect match for startups, which, due to limited resources, need all employees to work to maximum impact.

It isn't easy for an opinionated entrepreneur to step back and delegate the whole responsibility, especially at times where the entrepreneur can do the job both better and faster themselves. But investing the time in training people to be able to come up with solutions of their own is highly motivating for the employee whose career is now building speed, and it's the only way to ensure the entrepreneur does not become a bottleneck.

Perhaps the most critical element in creating a startup culture is being mission driven. A company on a mission can be as strong as a movement, driven forward by a passionate group of people in the shared urge to change things.

The startups that manage to articulate this clearly can create an almost cult-like atmosphere where the company becomes a major part of the employees' and founders' self-image. In this situation, employees wouldn't think to leave because they feel a part of a group, something bigger than themselves. They feel their contribution matters. Because the culture is clear, it snowballs stronger and stronger as people who don't fit in leave and are replaced by new ones that fit better. In the end, the people in the organization share values, have strong personal bonds, and dare to trust and rely on each other.

The above is a summary of something big and complicated, but my point is simple: I urge all tech startups to understand that the human element of building a strong company isn't a soft skill that's inferior to hard priorities such as coding and fundraising. Soft skills are, increasingly, a startup's best card. The world is changing, and the new generation of employees demand influence, flexibility, and meaning. That's our biggest opportunity.

Management, leadership, and communication take time, and time is a luxury you don't have in a startup. But it's not only something worth investing in, it's your best shot at making your company work. Today, the best talent wants to work somewhere where they make a difference, build something lasting, and get to solve problems. With a great culture, you can empower exactly that.

I'm not saying it's easy. I am saying it's worth it.

HAMPUS JAKOBSSON
The entrepreneur's guide to failing in a good way

Hampus Jakobsson (Sweden) has invested in more than 60 companies. He is the co-founder of TAT, which was on 12% of all mobile phones in 2010. He co-founded and is currently running The Ground and Nordic Makers. Jakobsson blogs at www.hajak.se.

Why the startup journey is more important than the destination

I never expected to be an entrepreneur. My first business, the mobile user interface (UI) company The Astonishing Tribe (TAT), was set up by six friends who wanted to work with something we loved and learn from our own mistakes rather than from others'. I am not even sure that it actually felt like a startup. TAT became a completely unexpected giant success both personally and financially (the business was bought by Blackberry for $150 million).

When I started my second business, I wanted more than financial success; it had to mean something to me.

I believe that an entrepreneur's true purpose is to try, learn, and experiment rather than follow more conventional ways of achieving success. Therefore, there is more room for failure, which is why in my eyes there are only four ways one can really fail as an entrepreneur. They are as follows:

- *Complete and utter personal bankruptcy*: If you take loans or borrow too much money from friends and family and don't succeed in financial terms—and a startup fails as a rule—it may mean that you and your nearest will be in a poor financial situation for a very long time. Avoid it.

- *Emotional/relational bankruptcy*: Some entrepreneurs ignore everything and everyone that doesn't contribute directly to their business's success. But remember, without your friends, family, or good health, you won't have success in anything. Sleep, eat (without a screen in front of you), and ensure that you meet every week with people who have nothing to do with the business.

- *Not trying hard enough*: If you don't put enough work into your business, you have no one to blame apart from yourself. You decide and you're responsible for your own choices.

- *Being an asshole*: Some founders become unpleasantly indifferent to how their business manages. They glorify venture capital and The Valley and decide that the only people who matter come from that world.

In 2000, I developed Crohn's disease and was in hospital for 6 months. When I was first admitted, I believed that the doctors were the wise ones. They hurried in for 10 minutes in smart doctors' white coats and pronounced judgment. But the people who actually saved me didn't wear these white coats. They were the nurses. Underpaid women with a short education to whom the doctors didn't show much respect.

The nurses who took care of me made me realize that it isn't always the most "skilled" or those with the highest status who contribute most, but those who listen, learn, and sincerely want to help. The nurses carried out most of the work, as is the case in a business where the employees do most of the hard work, while the bosses and the founders get all the credit and a hundredfold higher pay.

My simple point, therefore, is that if you preserve your health and your most important relations and value your employees instead of being an asshole, then you're already a success.

Starting a business is like lighting a bonfire. Most of the time you're trying to keep it going. You'll often make mistakes. You'll believe in things that few others will think possible—that people will rent out their homes to strangers or watch others play games online. On some days, it will feel like you're standing naked on a stage. Others will think you're crazy.

You will have doubts about yourself. Many doubts. I did in both of my startups. There will be days when everything is wonderful and mornings when you don't want to get out of bed.

Find local entrepreneurs with whom you can share your thoughts and feelings. They are your co- psychologists. Between you, you can build a team that you'll be glad to see every single day—people with whom it is pleasant to discuss and share the burdens. Understand that you won't be able to plan everything at the beginning. The only thing that has any importance in operational terms is learning from your users and building something scalable that serves them.

Entrepreneurship is difficult, but it is also a wonderful way of learning, of developing, and it may perhaps have a positive effect on the world. But it is rare that a startup grows large, becomes well known, or is looked on as a success by the rest of the world. The only way of being successful is therefore enjoying the journey just as much as the destination.

THEIS SØNDERGAARD
Trust everyone!

Theis Søndergaard (Denmark) is co-founder of Vivino—the world's most used wine app. He has been an entrepreneur since 2002, when he co-founded the software company BullGuard.

The following is a piece of really bad advice. If you follow it, there's a large risk that you'll be cheated, deceived, run over, and on the whole look like an idiot. I'd regret that, of course. But it *is* also really bad advice to urge good people to become entrepreneurs, as it's almost dead certain you'll fail. So if you nevertheless have taken the chance and thrown yourself into a new adventure, you may just as well place all your jetons on red and follow my advice: Trust everyone.

Trust is a mirror.

In 2002, I was a young, newly trained journalist with a blank CV and without much chance of a job in that branch. I therefore chose to change direction, and I called Morten Lund, a well-known Danish entrepreneur (co-founder of Skype), and asked if I could be his assistant. I'd worked a little for Morten while I was studying and I knew that he was always involved in crazy stuff. He said yes, and I subsequently worked around the clock for DKK 10,000 a month—moonlighting. We agreed that I owned 5% of all the projects he launched. That was our verbal agreement, and I never asked to have it in writing. It wasn't a deliberate choice, but I trusted (and trust) Morten 100%, so why waste time on it?

A year later, we worked together on building up BullGuard, which has since grown to 100 staff, DKK 120 million in turnover, and with me as CTO. It was a fantastic journey for me, and it even gave me a little nest egg that allowed me to move on to the next adventure, Vivino.

Could this have happened had I insisted on a written agreement? Perhaps. But trust works both ways; when you display trust, your partner's trust in you also grows, as does the wish to work closely together. BullGuard would quite definitely never have become a success without our close and trusting collaboration. Good marriages start with love, and nothing kills love faster than spending your first date dealing with paperwork. Talk things through and make agreements, that's OK, but if you don't trust your partner instinctively, find someone else.

Trust is oil.

If your business is an engine, trust is the oil, the lubricant you need to keep it running. Everything works more quickly when you display trust, and speed is decisive when you're an entrepreneur. Make your agreements by email and in your own words, and make it snappy. Otherwise, you'll spend vital time, money, and not least concern on uncovering risks unnecessarily. You already have 100 fundamental risks with your startup: Does your product work? Is your idea good? Have you chosen the right partner? and so on. Focus on the large challenges and deal with the problems as they arise.

At Vivino, we collaborated from the start with a small Swiss business, Kooaba, which we used for image recognition. The partnership was completely essential for ensuring our product worked; if they decided to close down their machine, nothing would work in Vivino. We had no contract with them for a long time, only an email; and when we finally, after a year, spent time making a contract, it was only two pages and most likely didn't cover many vital aspects. But we'd met Herbert and his partners several times and we trusted them.

When, a few years later, we raised money at Balderton Capital, their lawyers went through all our contracts (there weren't *that* many...) and said to us in dismay, If you read your homemade contract with Kooaba in a certain way, you could get the impression that Kooaba owned vital parts of Vivino. We should immediately make a new contract with Kooaba; indeed, if we didn't, then Balderton Capital would definitely not invest in us. We objected: Herbert would never think like that; it was absurd legalese. But we had to capitulate and make a new, 20-page contract. The point is, however, that we didn't need to do it until the time when we had the money and resources to do it and after we and Kooaba had established mutual trust.

Today, we're still using Kooaba for image recognition and Herbert has never cheated us. But now they've been bought by a large American company, so we'll surely have a new and even longer contract... *Groan!*

Trust is a growth hormone.

The easiest way to make a person 5 cm higher is to give her a task and tell her that you trust her completely to do it. If you display trust, everyone around you will grow, and the motivation for helping you will grow as well.

In my first business, BullGuard, it was difficult for me to trust the people around me to carry out their tasks without my help. Believing in my own genius, there could be no doubt that I could do things better. The result was an organization that didn't scale up, employees who didn't grow, and a worn-out boss (me) on the edge of a stress-provoked breakdown. Luckily, I learned to let go and display trust, in time.

During my working life, I have been the direct manager of about 200 people. They have an employment contract that states they must work 37 hours a week. I have never ever logged the hours of any employee, nor have I asked whether their day working at home was efficient. We run a business, not a kindergarten. Yes, for sure, some of them use the opportunity to relax once in a while, but that's OK; when you build a business together, you're running a marathon, not a 100 m sprint. You can choose to use your time on controls, or you can choose trust and release enormous resources among yourself and your employees to create value. If you trust that your employees want the best for you and your business, you increase the chance that they will—by a factor of 10.

Trust is luck.

One usually says that even the best idea, the best team, the best execution cannot succeed without a bit—or a lot—of luck. That's true, but luck can be cultivated, because trust and luck are two sides of the same coin. No one's become a millionaire in the lottery without having bought lottery tickets.

Once I had a consultation with a business psychologist, who fell off his chair when he saw the results of my personality test. It did say that I was a perfectionist, and with my work life it should have given me serious stress a long time ago. His test was undoubtedly correct, I do have plenty of perfectionistic traits, but I also trust blindly in my own luck. And if you do that, it's that much harder to be stressed, because—no matter how hard the odds are against me, how great the amount or pressure of work is—I can't imagine that it won't be successful in one way or another. And funnily enough, it nearly always is. An additional piece of advice is to work hard; golfers have much more luck the more they train.

Have I been cheated? Has my trust been abused? Absolutely, and most certainly more times than I am aware of. Suppliers have overinvoiced, partners have gone back on their word, employees have lied. That's part of life. But if, as a starting point, you trust that your fellow beings have good intentions, then it's my experience that it's a self-fulfilling prophecy. It's true enough; trust me.

THE BEST WAY TO FIND OUT IF YOU CAN TRUST SOMEBODY IS TO TRUST THEM.

Ernest Hemingway

CRAIG NEWMARK
Listen, act, repeat

Craig Newmark (United States) is the founder of craigslist and the Craig Newmark Philanthropies. He is a Web pioneer, a philanthropist, and a leading advocate on behalf of trustworthy journalism, veterans, military families, women in tech, and other civic and social justice causes.

Craig Newmark is the man behind craigslist—a website that today is among the 40 most visited websites in the world, is found in 70 countries, and can best be compared with Exchange and Mart in the United Kingdom.

Craig started craigslist back in 1995, and today he is reportedly worth more than DKK 3 billion. However, the last impression you get when talking to him is that of an entrepreneur guru. On the contrary, Craig is completely down to earth, something of a nerd (his word), and deeply passionate about using technology to make the world better.

He no longer heads craigslist but has dedicated his life to charitable work via Craig Newmark Philanthropies, which supports and connects nonprofit communities and drives powerful civic engagement.

As editor of this book, I talked to Craig about his craigslist past and his Craig Newmark Philanthropies present.

You started craigslist back in the 90s. How did you get the idea?

Actually I didn't. I had a number of ideas about how one could connect people and make a difference. I pitched them to my friends and my network, listened to their feedback, and acted on what they told me. The first thing I did was to listen to what others suggested and then I refined the best of their ideas and input. That's actually precisely the same method I follow today: listen, act, repeat.

You often hear good advice given to entrepreneurs that they must have a clear vision. It's vital that they also think about why they do what they do. But I read somewhere that you never had a vision for craigslist.

I certainly didn't have a single, clear vision with regard to transforming a single branch or the like. What drove me was a wish to build up communities, and that in fact turned out to be a very good vision.

At first glance, craigslist seems to be quite simple to copy as a concept. What was it that made it so unique that it has been more successful than its competitors?

It was our clear community values and a clear public announcement that we weren't doing it for the money. That was something we also followed in practice.

At Sunday school, I learned to assess when enough is enough and also that nobody needs a billion dollars.

Many young entrepreneurs probably find it difficult to visualize what it was like to be a tech entrepreneur in the 90s. How was it then compared to today?

There was quite clearly a greater consciousness of using technology to do something good for the community. Of course, there were also hard-as-nails capitalists, but there was another spirit, which is apparent in projects such as Wikipedia, for instance.

One often sees people like you, who suddenly become very rich, begin to do a lot of philanthropy. Why is that?

I don't really see it that way. Craigslist helped and helps the average citizen get food on his table, get a table, and find a roof to put the table under. That's not philanthropy, it's public service.

My project with Craig Newmark Philanthropies is a direct extension of this public service mission.

Today, you use most of your time working on Craig Newmark Philanthropies. What is the idea behind this project?

I have always supported a great number of different charitable organizations and projects. There was a time when I discovered that the money I used for this support was actually in something of a mess. I didn't know whom I supported or why. I therefore sought help to obtain a comprehensive view and then focus my efforts on the organizations I'm really fervent about helping. With Craig Newmark Philanthropies, I'm focused on trying to help the people and grassroots organizations that are "getting stuff done" in the areas of trustworthy journalism, women in tech, veterans and military families, voting rights and other areas.

On craigconnects, people therefore find organizations that are unbelievably effective and good at the things they do. They are honest, which unfortunately isn't always the case in the nonprofit world. And the website also enables people an opportunity to make direct contact with these organizations and take part in making a difference together with them.

What is a typical Craig day like?

Work and coffee.
Meetings at a local café.
Work at the office.
Coffee.
Maybe one more meeting.
Home to my wife, maybe watch some TV. I love TV.
Work.

And last: This interview will be included in *The GuruBook*, and *guru* means teacher or mentor, among other things. I've read that you describe yourself as a nonpracticing, secular Jew. Unlike many Americans, you don't get inspiration and values from your religion. Where do they come from then?

My rabbi is Leonard Cohen. He has been an influential poet and singer for almost 50 years, and he's my guru in the sense that he inspires me and gives me wisdom. It's Cohen's music that gets me through the day.

I can't run no more
With that lawless crowd,
Not while the killers
In high places
Say their prayers aloud.
But they've summoned
They've summoned
A big
Thundercloud.
They're going to hear from me.
—Leonard Cohen

THERE IS A CRACK IN
EVERYTHING, THAT'S HOW
THE LIGHT GETS IN.

Leonard Cohen

INNOVATION

INTRODUCTION

The GuruBook's second theme is *innovation*. This is a word that gets a lot of mileage in both the public and the private business community. Two tendencies seen repeatedly are the transition from phasing out to development and the transition from being ready for change to creating change—as a game-changer.

The contributors to this pillar of the book focus on how you turn new ideas into practice and generate results, to name some subjects. It is clear when you read the articles that innovation can vary in extent and impact. It can be a matter of radical and completely new initiatives, but it may as well take the shape of smaller, more limited, local innovations.

It is indisputable that innovation must generate value and that this can occur in many ways. In my work on *The GuruBook* I've come across an inspirational nursing home, where an effective innovative culture has succeeded in increasing efficiency, while this increased efficiency has at the same time released human resources that can now better meet the residents' individual needs. This was innovation with both target and meaning.

Enjoy yourself in this second pillar of the book, including the killing off of the *being ready for change* concept—a buzzword for many years. Readiness is a passive state in which you await the future. Successful innovators know that innovation is about being a game-changer. To act. To try things out. To be curious. To create.

When? Now!

TENDAYI VIKI
We train people to innovate and then tell them to stop doing so

Tendayi Viki (United Kingdom) is the founder and principal consultant at Benneli Jacobs and author of the bestseller *The Corporate Startup*. He has worked as a consultant for several companies including Pearson, Standard Bank, the World Bank, General Electric, and Whirlpool.

Bigger companies have a lot to learn from startups and vice versa.

One of the people in the world who knows most about this is entrepreneur, author, innovator, and former academic Tendayi Viki.

Tendayi has worked as a consultant, advisor, and coach for several large organizations including Airbus, Standard Bank, the British Museum, the World Bank, General Electric, Whirlpool, Tetrapak, and Pearson.

Tendayi co-designed Pearson's Lean Product Lifecycle, which is an innovation framework that won the Best Innovation Program 2015 at the Corporate Entrepreneur Awards in New York and Best Innovation Culture 2015 at the Corporate Entrepreneur Awards in London. Pearson is a London-based global education company with over 35,000 employees.

Tendayi has previously co-founded several companies including Tasksauce, Book Editions, and Research Innovations, and he has mentored and advised startups and innovation teams for Lean Startup Machine, the Startup Foundation, Founder's Hive, Rockstart Accelerator, and the Worldwide Web Foundation.

I asked Tendayi to draw on all of his experience and answer a few questions.

You expect that large companies will benefit a lot from the Lean Startup movement. Can you explain why?

Originally, the Lean Startup methodology was not designed for large companies. It was created by people like Steve Blank and Eric Ries to solve problems for startups, especially the challenges around premature scaling and therefore failing.

Lean Startup has developed into a powerful movement when it comes to understanding how to search and execute, and it offers some great tools that large companies can also benefit from.

For large companies, the reality might not be so much to search or execute but rather to search while executing. They have to focus on their core business and at the same time explore new business opportunities, and the key is to figure out how to balance this dual growth strategy.

Big companies know how to scale things, and they can plug new products and services into their scaling machine. However, the key questions are: When are you ready to scale? When have we tested the product enough and in the right way?

The answer is to move back a couple of steps and ask yourself: Do we have a real customer need? Have we created a viable solution? And do we have the right business model to deliver on that need?

If the answer is yes to these three questions, then you're ready to scale, and Lean Startup gives you the tools that you need to start asking these questions.

A lot of the time, you'll hear lean startups mentioning the importance of failing cheap and fast, but I don't really see that mindset working in a bigger organization.

The interesting thing it that Lean Startup is not really about cheap or fast but about doing the right thing at the right time. The startup community often confuses bootstrapping with lean.

You can use a lot of different tools for this process of discovering when you have to create a viable solution. In some cases, prototyping can work—in others, design thinking or minimum viable products. The key is to test your ideas before you scale. Sometimes you do this just by an interview, other times it's a landing page, and sometimes it might be building a version of the product. It all depends on the risky assumptions you are testing and where you are in your innovation journey.

You have some principles for building innovation ecosystems in established companies. What are these?

In our book *The Corporate Startup*, my co-authors and I present five principles around this.

I've discovered that a lot of large companies study the Lean Startup, train their teams to use it, and then the teams go back to work in the company. However, the problem is that they're not going back to a startup. They're going back to the same organization that works in a different way from what they have just learned. So the same manager who sent them to training now tells them to stop doing experiments and write a 30-page business plan.

Should innovation units then be physically separate from the core business?

It depends. What is the company? What is the environment like? It's not like you're hiding. You appear as line time in the budget each year, so even if you're building things separately, you still have to align with the goals of your separate division and with the company's overall mission, vision, goals, and budgets.

I know that you're also quite critical when it comes to this idea of "acting like startups."

Innovation is now the main strategic priority in most companies. The majority of executives indicate a need for their companies to develop sustainable innovation processes. However, when seeking advice on what to do, managers are often told that their companies should start "acting like startups." This "sage" advice has resulted in the proliferation of idea competitions and innovation labs, where innovation theatre rather real innovation takes place. The success of these innovation labs has been patchy at best, with very few successful new products.

If acting like startups is not the right mindset or method, then what is?

Large companies are not startups, nor should they strive to be. While startups focus on searching for profitable business models, most large companies are executing on an already successful business model that is generating revenues and profits. This means that large companies are faced with the perennial question of how to execute or exploit the currently successful business model while simultaneously searching for or exploring new opportunities for future growth. This has always been a challenge for established companies, but the pace of change in the modern economy now makes these challenges even more pressing.

So rather than acting like startups, large companies need to build innovation ecosystems. These ecosystems will contain core products currently generating revenues and innovative new products that are aimed at the future. The company has to be world class at managing both types of products and using the right methods for innovation. This means that companies need to understand the elements that are involved in creating an innovation ecosystem—from the strategic lens to incremental investing and day-to-day product development best practices.

Managing innovation is therefore key?

Every company should have a clear strategy for their innovation efforts. This strategy should be based on taking a point of view about where the world is going, what are the key trends affecting our business, and how we are going to use innovation to respond. This is the case whether you're a small or big company. You need to be able to clearly tell your staff where they should invest their energy when it comes to innovation. This is an innovation thesis. This enables you to clearly discuss whether new product ideas are an expression of this strategy or not.

Finally, you should ask more questions. For instance: Do we have enough transformational innovation and disruptive innovation in our organization? When we look at our innovation portfolio, is there a gap between our strategy and what we actually do?

You also talk about the importance of innovation accounting.

Yes. The point is, What is the right thing to do at the right time? This is the practice we want our product teams to engage in. So to support this work, our investment decisions should be based on asking the right questions at the right time. Rather than ask for long business cases, we can use incremental investing. Start with small investments and then double down our resources on those projects that are showing the most promise and traction.

How do you envision the companies of the future? Will they be a hybrid between startups and big corporations?

I don't know, to be honest, but I know that companies are going to have to change the way they work. They have to become more responsive. Companies of the future should be highly collaborative, work with startups and universities, and co-create with customers. I think this will require companies to decrease the distance between the CEO and the customers, and I think that companies are going to have to break down their silos and become more cross-functional.

A DISCOVERY IS SAID TO BE AN ACCIDENT MEETING A PREPARED MIND.

A. von Szent-Gyorgyi

SALIM ISMAIL
We are animals with tools

Salim Ismail (Canada) is a serial entrepreneur, angel investor, author, and technology strategist. He is best known as the founding executive director of Singularity University and lead author of *Exponential Organizations*. In March 2017, he was added to the board of the XPRIZE Foundation.

When I (Jonathan) read the book *Exponential Organizations* 3 years ago, a whole new world opened up for me. Up until then, I didn't know Salim Ismail that well—just like a lot of other people, I guess.

Today, Salim Ismail is one of the hottest names in the business world. He has spent the last 7 years building Singularity University as its founding executive director and current global ambassador. Prior to that, Ismail was vice president at Yahoo, where he built and ran Brickhouse, the company's internal incubator. His last company, Ångströ, a news aggregation startup, was sold to Google in 2010.

Salim Ismail has founded and/or operated seven early-stage companies, including PubSub Concepts, which laid some of the foundation for the real-time Web, and the New York Grant Company, in direct response to 9/11. In its first year, the organization attracted over 400 clients and delivered over $12 million of federal grants to the local economy.

I'm fascinated by Salim's way of thinking, and I wanted to get to know this passionate businessman and entrepreneur better. We sat down for a chat, and of course we started by talking about his Amazon number-one bestseller *Exponential Organizations*…

In your book you write that we struggle to understand exponentiality as human beings. What does this concept mean, and why is that?

Have a look at this figure:

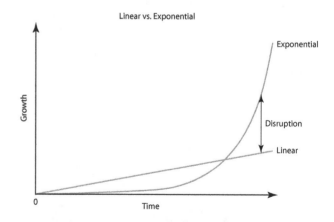

Linear vs. Exponential

The linear growth is how we normally perceive the world and business. If you want to move from one place to another, you could calculate your way of getting there into a number of steps. For instance, 30 normal steps. You have then understood the linear development from A to B.

However, exponentiality is something different and hard to grasp for the human mind. If I take 30 doubling steps—1, 2, 4, 8, 16, and so on—at step 30, I've gone a billion meters. I'm 26 times around the world, which is a little bit further than a 30-meter stretch, and it's hard to gauge where I'd be one-third or two-thirds of the way.

Why is that hard for our brains to grasp?

We have evolved over 4 billion years—to survive and to co-create. We are basically animals with tools, and our DNA is very close to that of gorillas.

This also means that our brains are programmed in a local and linear way. All of our senses work through incremental steps, and all of our education and training is incremental and based on local materials.

This means that we are cognitively bad at spotting exponential growth, because it goes against our senses, against our biology.

How do you transcend biology then?

You have to understand the doubling patterns of exponential growth. We live in a unique time where we're experiencing doubling patterns in tech, neuroscience, bitcoins, biotech, drones, 3D printing, and so on. The doubling patterns are faster and faster. With drones, for instance, the growth pattern doubles every 9 months.

And a doubling pattern is what?

The doubling pattern was identified by Gordon Moore in Moore's Law. Once the doubling pattern starts, it doesn't stop. We use current computers to design faster computers, which then build even faster computers, and so on. Let me give you an example...

Ten years ago, we had 500 million internet-connected devices. Today, there are about 15 billion. By 2020, there will be 50 billion, and a decade later, we'll have a trillion internet-connected devices as we literally information enable every aspect of the world in the internet of things (IoT). Think about that for a second. The internet is now the world's nervous system, with our mobile devices serving as edge points and nodes in that network.

We like to think that 30 or 40 years into the Information Revolution we are well along in terms of its development. But according to this metric, we're just 1% of the way down the road.

You combine this doubling pattern development with the idea of information enabling.

Yes. The driver fueling this development is information. Once any domain, discipline, technology, or industry becomes information enabled and powered by information flows, its performance begins doubling approximately annually.

Several key technologies today are now information enabled and following the same trajectory—for instance, artificial intelligence, robotics, neuroscience, data science, and nanotechnology.

What does this mean for our society and the different industries?

One example could be transportation.

In the current reality, we roughly buy one car per family. You take x number of trips per family, and sometimes you invest in two cars.

However, with current developments in the self-driving industry, solar technology, and the IoT, we will have a completely different scenario in a few years from now.

Imagine a near future where I can access a small solar-powered car just by going to the next street, where it's parked, after someone else has just used it. This will change the supply side and the market, and the nature of demand will change.

Today, Manhattan has 13,000 taxis and 120,000 private cars. If you power the cars using solar energy, make them self-driving, and combine this with the IoT, you can meet the same needs in an area like Manhattan with just 9000 cars. And you would only have to wait 36 seconds for your next car to arrive. Today, people are waiting 10 or more minutes to get a taxi.

This means that you transform the market from scarcity to abundance.

That doesn't sound like good news for the car industry.

Last year, 85 million cars were sold in the United States. My estimate is that we need to sell 10%–15% of that. What do we need 20 car companies for? We've seen this in the music industry with iTunes and Spotify. So you're right in the sense that the car companies definitely need to start innovating on their business models.

Can you briefly describe the difference between incremental innovation and the kind of disruptive innovation that's fueled by exponentials?

The features and performance of my car improve incrementally at about 2% a year. In fact, most innovation at big companies is incremental. Cleaning products get slightly better or "new and improved" in a linear fashion over time. Over the past few decades, cars have been getting slightly better gas mileage year to year, go slightly faster, and are marginally safer. Even the electric car is still an incremental innovation on the concept of a car.

Autonomous cars, on the other hand, are truly disruptive because they take the driver out of the equation completely with the help of robotics, sensors, artificial intelligence (to route and analyze information), and other exponentials. For the first time in 100 years, Moore's Law is hitting transportation. All of a sudden, we have "intelligent" cars that can park themselves. The next generation of autonomous cars will drive in bumper-to-bumper traffic, navigate complicated street environments, and so on. The pace of change in cars is moving very fast, indeed, because of information enablement.

Are there any industries other than transportation that will experience the same?

Yes absolutely. One could be the food industry.

Today, an average meal in the United States travels 4000 km to get to my table. If I start growing tomatoes at local farms, then I do not need vegetables from 4000 km away. This will save transportation and energy costs. Technology can help us get there.

Another example that you use is Nokia and the community-based traffic and navigation app Waze.

Yes. So Nokia, after the iPhone was announced in a "big bet," bought Navtech, which owns all the circular traffic sensors on all the roads in 35 countries or so, and they were figuring they would protect themselves against… By having real-time traffic information and owning the source. At the same time, Waze launched, which piggybacks on your GPS, and 5 years later, Nokia has essentially gone out of business. They get sold for less than what they paid for in Navtech, and Waze gets sold for a billion dollars, and they had 50 million traffic points because every single GPS, and of course, that's excluding exponentially.

It's probably up to about 100 million today. There was therefore a great indication of a few "bank on" physical assets than somebody who was doing the same thing with the digital environment or an information-based environment will surpass you very, very quickly.

At Singularity University, you work with this mindset and try to solve some of the world's largest problems.

Our education mission is to educate the world's leaders that this is happening. We then try to enable them to solve big problems such as pandemics or climate change—real exponential problems. For instance, Ebola is expanding at a doubling rate, so you can't solve it with a linear solution.

We want to make sure that all business leaders wake up and realize the exponentiality of the problems and figure out ways of solving them.

And your book *Exponential Organizations* is part of this mission?

Yes. The mission of my book is to explain how to organize this process, what kinds of organizational structures do we need going forward?

Exponential organizations are governed by an assumption of abundance—unlike linear organizations that are necessarily constrained by limited resources.

Hyatt, for example, is a typically linear organization—which isn't to say that it isn't also hugely successful. With hundreds of locations in dozens of countries, Hyatt is one of the most widely recognized hotel chains in the world.

But each time it wants to open a new location, Hyatt needs to build a new hotel or buy a preexisting property. It needs to hire cooking, cleaning, and administrative staff. It needs to pay for renovations and maintenance, and any number of other periodic issues that may arise.

Growth is obviously possible within that framework, but it proceeds deliberately and, often, painstakingly, in a roughly linear fashion.

By contrast, Airbnb, the popular short-term real estate rental market, is designed for rapid, almost effortless growth. Its low organizational demands are inversely proportional to its huge business potential. Airbnb doesn't own any property, but it has already accumulated over 1 million listings in more than 34,000 cities, and has been valued at $20 billion.

DANNY LANGE
Becoming truly data driven

Danny Lange (Denmark) is vice president of AI and machine learning at Unity Technologies. Previously, Lange was head of machine learning at Uber, where he led the efforts to build a highly scalable machine learning platform to support all parts of Uber's business from the Uber app to self-driving cars.

Danny Lange might not be a name that rings a bell among most leaders, innovators, and entrepreneurs, but it really ought to in the future. Why? Because Lange is the brain behind building the machine learning and artificial intelligence (AI) efforts at Amazon, Uber, and currently Unity Technologies.

Danny was head of machine learning at Uber, where he led an effort to build its machine learning platform. Before, he was the general manager of Amazon Machine Learning—an Amazon Web Services product that offers machine learning as a service.

This impressive and inspiring background made me reach out to Danny to do an interview about his thoughts around the present and future of machine learning and AI—two of the most interesting and disruptive technologies in the world currently.

You used to work as head of machine learning at Uber. How did Uber work with AI and machine learning?

Uber is a business that is entirely data driven—just like Amazon, where I worked previously.

At Uber, they focus on metrics and measurements. I was involved in all three business units at Uber—the core business, the mapping business, and the self-driving car business.

In the core business, we used machine learning to estimate the time of arrival, pairing people up for Uber pool rides and improving the pickup experience by having a computer learn over time where the good pickup spots are in a particular city.

Basically, the core function of the machine learning algorithms is to measure the experience and minimize the friction during a pickup. For instance, in the United States, there are a lot of situations and places in which an Uber vehicle cannot stop. We designed a system that learned this and thus was able to offer a problem-free experience by suggesting both driver and customer meet 20–30 yards away from where the car was booked to stop in the app.

So machine learning was and is all about reducing friction?

Not only, but at Uber it was a big part of the philosophy. In the second business, the mapping business, we used machine learning to build maps for the drivers. We made a system that could read street signs and populate the map. This means that where most companies and people build maps by hind, we used machine learning for the same purpose.

As with the core business, the benefit from doing it like this is that you develop a system that keeps learning and improving. Rather than building a system where you constantly have to update it manually or calculate all possible outcomes, we have a system that learns by itself and continues to improve—without us having to do more than support it a little on the side.

Could a company like Uber have existed before we had machine learning?

It could to some extent, but not at the scale and quality of service we see now.

In the old days, we would have had to base the product on insights and intelligence—built up by people. This could create an okay product but never compete with the current pickup experience, where the system bases its suggestions on millions of rides every day. Just like Uber's third business unit, the self-driving car business, the idea is to use machine learning to constantly improve the experience. With the self-driving cars, it can be used to detect objects, plan the optimal route, make predictions about bicycles, and so on.

For people that don't really understand machine learning, what is the idea behind it, and what are the possibilities in the future?

It's all in the data and in capturing the patterns. That is what the systems are doing.

Let me explain to you how it works. Imagine that you have to build an application that predicts the shipping time for a company. In the old days, you would look at it the following way: There is a place where you pick up the package and a destination address. You then have to build up a complicated set of rules, a rule system, to include the speed of the trucks, planes, delays, and so on. You would try to compute it and maybe end up with two or three hundred rules to try to predict the shipping time.

In machine learning, you don't think or work like this. Instead, you will base your system on millions of package deliveries that have already been made; this is the most important thing—your data. Within this data you will have the weekdays, the sizes of the packages, how quickly they were delivered, and so on. Within machine learning you call this the *ground truth*.

So, *ground truthing* refers to the process of gathering the proper objective, provable data for the test. For example, Bayesian spam filtering is a common example of this. In this system, the algorithm is manually taught the differences between spam and nonspam. This depends on the ground truth of the messages used to train the algorithm; inaccuracies in the ground truth will correlate to inaccuracies in the resulting spam/nonspam verdicts.

In the case of the shipping, you will then have millions of packages delivered, and the computer can learn a statistical model. When you feed in a new delivery, the system will use the statistics to predict the shipping time based on history.

What we have learned is that this system will always outperform the rule-based system. We have stopped trying to understand the rules. Instead, we leave it to the machine learning system to do that.

Instead of having to maintain the rules manually, you leave it to the machine learning algorithm to do so. Correct?

Yes, and since the world is constantly changing, this will improve the predictions a lot and save a lot of manpower and time. In the case of machine learning, you can monitor the feedback and constantly measure how good your model is.

Is that the same as AI, which is another hot technology and trend at the moment?

To me, artificial intelligence is about how a system is being perceived and how a system presents itself.

If you look at predicting shipping time, that is not really intelligence. But when you start taking an entire organization and have everything it does—from predicting shipping times to detecting hazard materials with computer vision, self-driving trucks, dynamic prizing based on demand, and so on—it actually appears pretty smart and intelligent to me.

That was our philosophy at Amazon: that the whole company would start appearing more intelligent to the customer. And at one point, we could actually claim that we were a really smart organization.

We've been talking for AI for a long time, but it hasn't really drastically changed industries and business models yet. When will this happen, do you think?

That is a huge shift underway. Of course, not everyone can be Amazon, but we can all learn from them.

In the case of Amazon, their mindset is that they need to be able to beat every retailer out there. They do this by knowing you better. Getting you things faster. Giving you more reasonable prices. Offering you more than a billion products. And all of this is only possible by integrating machine learning and AI into every aspect of the business and business model.

Uber is the same. They can run out of San Francisco but beat a taxi company in almost every country. Well, at least where they are legal. Both companies are using the technology to a scale that has never been seen before. It enables them to run a service in a far away country better than the people actually living in the country.

We're seeing a development where you will be in trouble 24–36 months from now if you don't start taking machine learning seriously. It will happen especially in industries such as transportation, shipping, finance, and retail, but all kinds of companies and leaders should look into this much deeper.

Of course, the big companies have an advantage due to the amount of data they often have. The startups lack this, and data is increasingly becoming king.

For example, you may be able to build a better app with a better backend than Uber, and pay a crew of drivers more money, but if you don't have the data to deliver a consistently better pickup experience, all of that might not matter at all.

So you have to be Uber or Amazon to succeed?

Fortunately not, but you have to start collecting data and working with machine learning.

Imagine that you're a company building houses. There will be many examples—a shipping company without shipping data. A lot of startups are running into the problem that they don't have the data. Currently, we build homes and offices based on the architect's creativity and our history and experience of building houses. However, in the future, we could use data and AI to totally change the way we think about the design of houses.

At an artificial space like Unity, where I work with gaming universes, you could build and simulate a family living in that house. You can build virtual characters to live in the house. You can accelerate and have thousands of families living in the house virtually for a year but calculate the results in weeks.

You can then ask your system to figure out how the experience was. Is the hallway too narrow? Was there enough room for furniture? When we sit down and watch TV, where do we prefer the TV to be placed?

By having virtual people living in these homes, we can optimize home building for emotional optimization.

Really? Virtual people are testing products and services before they are launched?

Yes. And in numbers that would never be possible in the real world and without the risk of actually building the wrong product.

It sounds a bit like crazy magic!

It's not. It's just applied machine learning. It's coming to us now because of the development in computing power.

If you look at the growth in computer power, it's currently going through the roof. In the old days, smart people would try to create such models in their head and implement them in highly efficient programming languages.

They would be highly efficient implementations, but always approximations. This paradigm has changed.

And in addition to this, growth in computer power data is growing rapidly too, right?

Indeed. You have to remember that it's only 10 years ago that the first iPhone was released.

Before then, nobody captured your location. Now everything captures your location and everything else.

This means that today we have all this data.

You also talk about the concept of *reinforcement learning*, where data is also vital.

Yes, and reinforcement learning is actually what I spend most of my time on. In traditional machine learning, you work with the concept of the ground truth. In reinforcement learning, you let the system learn the truth itself.

You provide the system with some very fundamental guidelines. We call those *rewards*.

We then provide the system with some ethics. Tell it what is good and bad. For example, getting run over by a car is bad, and getting to a destination in time is good. That is it—a very fundamental and low-level set of rules.

The system will now experiment its way toward perfection. The key thing is that there is no algorithm dictating traffic law. The system will automatically aim to not kill people and get there in time.

These systems can learn very complex things. If we talk about poker, they can learn to start bluffing—learn to fool you, make some moves that will basically hide the real intention. So these systems build strategic behavior and do things that work—at a very high rate, figure out these subtle strategies.

Going back to the Amazon and Uber cases, these companies might have all that data, but a normal retail store does not?

Correct, but I envision a development where cloud services will be made available to everybody, and in these services, things like face recognition and machine learning will be included.

This means that a physical retail shop can use that cloud service to recognize and track every customer coming into their store, the moment you step into their chain of clothing stores. If they can recognize your face, the employee will know your name, what you looked at last time, what you prefer, and so on.

Staff will be able to give you personal assistance, and I think that this development may actually change the dynamics once again and might revolutionize the space of retail. So machine learning and AI is fundamentally changing the way that things are working around us.

What is your advice to leaders and companies reading this? How should they navigate this field in the future?

It's about culture more than projects. Stop creating projects and test projects. Instead, think about how machine learning and AI can fundamentally change how you are working and innovating.

Also try looking at other industries and what you can learn from them. For example, at my current job at Unity Technologies, our gaming world is actually much more than just gaming.

What we work with is real simulations of an artificial world. When you play a game, it doesn't really exist in reality.

You can use the same methodology in other industries. If you're building a self-driving vehicle, it can be very dangerous to drive around on real streets to test the vehicle. Instead, you could create a virtual street scenario and train the vehicles in this. You put in pedestrians, parked cars, intersections and so on, and the machine learning algorithm in the car will then in fact be able to train real-world action in a virtual space.

So I would advise most companies to change their mindset and become truly data driven.

IT IS A CAPITAL MISTAKE TO THEORIZE BEFORE ONE HAS DATA.

Sherlock Holmes

ALF REHN
The land of lost ambition

Alf Rehn (Finland) is an internationally recognized business thinker and has taught at universities all over the globe. He has been called an "enfant terrible of organization studies," while *The Times* named him a "star of the future."

I know that Alf Rehn doesn't like being referred to as a Finnish superstar of the future, but I use these words anyway because I was very inspired by our conversation around creativity, innovation, and what Rehn calls "the land of lost ambition." I hope you find it inspiring too.

I know that you don't like the idea of the "singular genius." Could you please tell me more about why? And if creativity doesn't come from the individual, where does it come from?

I talk about *creative cultures*, and I do so as a way to get away from the cult of the individual in the thinking around creativity.

We're far too focused on the notion of the singular genius coming up with a singular idea, when the real issue of creativity—particularly in organizations—is how we can create a fertile environment for ideas, one where they are engaged with, nurtured, and cared for. This also means that creative cultures are attentive to ideas from *all* their members, not just the few who've been designated as the "creative ones."

What sets these kinds of cultures apart from the not-so-creative cultures?

They are more creative, more innovative, and more adept at managing change. Whereas a lot of the discussion about creativity in an organization still focuses on individuals and their ideas, I've tried to show that even a hypercreative individual will flounder in an organization that lacks care and nurturing when it comes to ideas, and that cultures tend to be far better at killing ideas than they are at taking care of them.

So, you could say that the notion of creative cultures refers to what happens after ideation, when an idea meets the cold, hard glare of reality. Will the culture scoff, laugh, or yawn at it? Will the culture engage or tell the progenitor of the idea why it won't work? Will the culture nurture new ideas like you'd nurture a child—one not yet mature but with tremendous potential?

For me, this is what sets some cultures apart. Not that they talk the talk about creativity. Not that they're great at brainstorming. Rather, that they are good at things like care and nurturing, support and succor. The weird thing is, if you're good at such soft things, the world will reward you with cold, hard cash.

I like the idea that being good at soft things rewards you with harder things. But why do some companies tend to destroy their own creativity?

By and large, companies are good at seeing the value of their history and terrible at seeing the potential value in the people. Companies tend to be very locked in to the things that made them great, and without knowing it, very wedded to the notion that their future should look very much like their past. This means that when they start exploring new opportunities, they unconsciously limit their creative space.

So, a company can have a tremendous amount of creative potential but limit itself by only allowing ideas and experiments that stick closely to what has historically worked for it. Further, a company might pay lip service to innovation, while at the same time only looking at familiar opportunities. Simply put, it isn't enough for a company just to "get creative," it also needs to be able to critically review what kind of creativity and what kind of innovation it has tended to allow.

So creativity doesn't come naturally to us. What can we do about it as individuals, as leaders, and as organizations?

Simply put, our brain is lazy and so are we. It is always easier to go with what one already knows, using well-honed routines and acquired experience. Creativity requires extra energy, and true creativity may even require that we unlearn some things and learn completely new ones. All of this comes at a cost, which is why we often subconsciously turn away from creative thoughts—particularly very creative ones. The funny/scary thing is that our brain can actually trick us into believing that we're being creative when we're actually just using old knowledge and known processes.

To work around this, I often suggest people start exploring their own discomfort. Look at the ideas you ignore or say no to and ask yourself *why* you ignored them. Sometimes it might simply be because the ideas weren't very good, but often it can be about how new ideas seem to require too much work from us. Understanding this, our occasional discomfort with novelty, can then be harnessed to learn new forms of ideation.

Speaking of new forms of ideation, you have the concept of a *dangerous idea*. What is that?

Oscar Wilde might have said it best: "An idea that is not dangerous is unworthy of being called an idea at all." I sort of riff on that, and in my book *Dangerous Ideas*, I argued that too much of what is presented as "creativity" are in fact quite safe and tepid ideas. Instead, I said, we should look for ideas that make people angry, disgusted, creeped out. Ideas that make people laugh at us, spit in our faces, threaten legal action. If everyone likes your idea, it can't be very good; you've not challenged anyone. If your idea makes people furious, you're on to something.

You're writing a book called *Saving Innovation*, and at the same time you claim that having more innovation books isn't necessarily better. You'll have to explain that to me!

Hey, I wrote a creativity book about why there are too many creativity books! This just follows suit… Heh! No, it's a good question. What I've tried to argue is that a great deal of the innovation literature is rather uninnovative. Most innovation books look just like all the others, using the same examples and prescribing the same solutions. They also tend to be very bad at looking more critically at innovation, and instead merely present the same shiny, happy stories as everyone else.

What I wanted to write about was how innovation can be lost and squandered, and about how the innovation industry—all us gurus, consultants, and writers—are part of the problem. I'm arguing that innovation has been turned into a bullshit buzzword, and that people who write books about it need to take a long, hard look at themselves and ask whether we're really supporting innovation as a meaningful driver of human advancement or just a fancy word we use to enrich ourselves.

When you write about innovation, you also write about "the land of lost ambition." What is that?

Once upon a time, innovation stood for "What miracles can we achieve?!" Today, many companies see it as just something to churn out. It doesn't matter if it's a real innovation or if it creates significant, valuable change. It only matters that you have something, anything, that can be referred to as an innovation in the PR material. So yes, I believe that many companies lack ambition in their innovation endeavors. As long as it is new, and as long as you can refer to it as an innovation, managers are happy.

But this has a dark side. Innovation is still the single best chance we have to create things to solve the many wicked problems of our planet. While companies should be thinking about things like the water crisis, global warming, social inequality, and the cataclysmic shifts of demography, many are still far too caught up in questions like "Should we create an app?" and "Can we put more smart sensors into our socks/shovels/shawarma?" Innovation should be ambitious. These days, however, only a small fraction of what is called "innovation" actually is.

TO THE PERSON WHO DOES NOT
KNOW WHERE HE WANTS TO GO
THERE IS NO FAVORABLE WIND.

Seneca

JULIE KJÆR-MADSEN
Curiosity is an irritating, underestimated driving force

Julie Kjær-Madsen (Denmark) is an innovation specialist and owner of the Loop Company. She is also a master practitioner in concept making and business innovation and has previously worked at KOMPAN, LEGO, and Danfoss Universe.

The future belongs to the curious.

We will measure curiosity in the future just as we measure the ability to innovate. In our organizations today, we use the word *innovation* in many contexts. We say we want to be innovative. That's relatively easy to say but much more difficult to be. The ability to innovate can nevertheless be strengthened by cultivating curiosity. That is the key we need.

To be curious is to be interested and greedy for knowledge. We are born with curiosity. As children, we examine everything we can get our hands on. We take things to pieces, find out what they're made of, how they're put together, and how they work. We create for ourselves an understanding of the world through our curiosity. As long as we're children.

Daniel Goleman states the following in his book *Emotional Intelligence*:

A child's readiness for school depends on the most basic of all knowledge, how to learn. The report lists the seven key ingredients of this crucial capacity—all related to emotional intelligence. One of these is Curiosity. The sense that finding out about things is positive and leads to pleasure.

The innovative organization is *irritatingly* curious. It stops and examines contexts; it turns things upside down, dissects challenges, and looks at them from many angles. The curious organization uses the constructive question mark: What if? What if one could? How could we? Who should we involve? Where is the knowledge we can use? The curious organization solves problems by looking at them with constructive wonder. The constant changing of time requires that we learn to be curious. This is irritatingly time-consuming—and very, very underestimated.

Curiosity must be reinvented.

Curiosity is connected with something negative. Although we are born curious, we are brought up to not be curious. On the contrary.

The Constant Questioner gets a slap and is sent to bed because he's curious. Curious George gets into all sorts of potentially dangerous situations because he's seduced by his curiosity. The Constant Questioner should stop asking all those "stupid" questions, and Curious George should rein in his curiosity. The message is that curiosity makes problems for us. Being curious is not associated with anything positive. It's mainly perceived as something a little improper. The curious pries. The curious is ignorant; he doesn't know the answer.

Here's the rub: We're brought up to be clever. When we're clever, we know the answer. We know what we're examined in. We understand, can explain, and can answer. The clever employee knows the answer. His answer isn't "What if…?"

The public rhetoric isn't about curiosity but about reaching a conclusion. Politicians are required to give answers, and they give them in a cocksure way. The media reach conclusions. This is the context and this is why. Bang. That's the way it is. Over and done with.

Imagine if asking good questions was held in high esteem. Imagine if being able to formulate visionary "what if" questions was widely recognized. As a politician, as a journalist—and as an employee.

Employees who question decisions are not cooperative. They don't have the right attitude. If we ask organizations working with innovation what their greatest challenge is, the answer is often, It is difficult to implement something new. That deep-rootedness is the greatest challenge. It's obvious. We don't give the members of the organization the chance to come to an understanding of changes. We haven't included curiosity in the equation. It's as if we still think that change is a matter of management and communication as determined by the situation. Imagine if we more often asked for curious exploitation of all that we want to change and anchor. If we invited the organization to use curiosity in solving the challenges and qualifying the decisions.

Curiosity: it's something we practice!

We must facilitate curiosity. Use it. Until we *are* curious naturally, we must ensure that we practice it and use curiosity. Applied curiosity is a discipline. It's something that's easy to forget in our everyday evidence-based and reflective thinking processes. What does being curious as part of an innovation process mean? How do you do it?

When we work with problem-solving or innovation processes, where there's a need to identify new areas of opportunities, we can consciously practice curiosity. There are many ways of working with curiosity in a divergent way of thinking. What is important is that we consciously try to unfold the subject in various directions and look at things constructively. One of the methods is called *untangling*.

As an illustration, let us try to *untangle* a cupcake. If we look at a cupcake with curious eyes, it comprises many things. There are the ingredients, the various glazes and decorations, the form they're baked in, the recipes, the dishes and cake stands specially made for cupcakes. But it is also the process of baking them. Baking and decorating them can be a social activity; perhaps they're being baked for a social event, and finally, it could be that they're being baked so we can show the final results on Facebook. There are "I would like" cakes and "I shouldn't eat cake" cakes. There's a cupcake trend. There are the logistics, packaging, shipping, foodstuff approvals, and a whole lot more. Different eyes will look at things from different angles. And now we can think about what it is that we've created a view of. Ingredients and packaging. Dilemmas and social needs. Production and trends. Much, much more than just a cupcake.

That you are facilitated through an exercise that turns something you know well on its head is often regarded as something very valuable and exciting. It creates awareness that there are many other solutions to the question you're working on and many more angles to look at it from. They are the exercises that create the greatest understanding of what innovation really is.

The innovative organization can use curiosity to work with changes and the anchoring of something new. If we turn the process around and refrain from communicating what it is that we want anchored, but instead involve our employees, who will help anchor something new in an open and curious process, then we can qualify and develop new solutions that to a greater extent build on the experiences, knowledge, and resources in the organization. What does the change I am a part of mean? How can I dissect it, understand it, qualify it, and put it together again? How can I add my knowledge and experience to it and place it in the reality that I know, where I am the specialist and where it must function every day?

Curiosity becomes the key to successful anchoring.

One, two, three, curiosity.

There's only one thing to do: get curiosity rolling! That requires conscious decision and action.

- *Use rhetoric*: Use the word *curiosity* to describe positive behavior and ways of thinking. Find visible solutions and new angles that arise through the conscious use of curiosity. Mention curiosity as a behavior or way of thought that generates value.
- *Recognize curiosity*: Point out curiosity in the organization. Make it clear that curiosity is a valued ability. Ensure you put into words how the combination of knowledge and a curiosity-driven adaptation of knowledge creates results. Honor curiosity. Hire curiosity.
- *Plan curiosity*: Put it on the agenda. Create room for curious processes at meetings and workshops and in everyday work. Include methods involving curiosity in work processes.
- *Be good at being curious*: Train the staff. Learn it. Facilitate curiosity training.

You cannot be curious if you think you know the answer.

Let's create the framework for showing the original definition of curiosity: Curiosity is an inborn motivation and urge to examine something closely, accompanied by information-seeking behavior, which results in a better understanding of a given area and gradually diminishes what the unusual in it is. Let us recognize curiosity as the key to innovation and cultivate it as a natural driving force.

THE CURE FOR BOREDOM IS CURIOSITY. THERE IS NO CURE FOR CURIOSITY.

Dorothy Parker

PAUL NUNES
The innovator's disaster

Paul Nunes (United States) is the global managing director of the Accenture Institute for High Performance. He is a well-known business author, patent holder, and a frequent and sought-after speaker on the topic of business strategy. His research has been featured in publications worldwide, including *The New York Times, The Wall Street Journal, USA Today*, and Forbes.com.

It used to take years or even decades for disruptive innovations to dethrone dominant products and services. But now, any business can be devastated virtually overnight by something better and cheaper. Here's how executives can harness the power of this new type of innovation.

When Google launched its free navigation app Google Maps Navigation, the company was looking simply to drive more eyeballs to more advertisements by integrating more already-digital information. But from the outset, the app outperformed expensive, standalone GPS devices on every strategic dimension. It was, and continues to be, lower cost (i.e., free); highly differentiated, as it is updated and enhanced in real time; and more customer-friendly, as it connects with other smartphone apps, including search results, maps, mail, and contacts.

Little surprise, then, that the major players in the GPS device market lost as much as 85% of their market capitalization in the 18 months after the introduction of Google Maps. The lesson learned: today's innovations come out of left field, combining technologies seemingly unrelated to a company's offerings, to achieve a dramatically better value proposition.

Markets are being rocked by this new kind of offering, and word of their superiority in all relevant dimensions now travels the globe in a flash. As a result, entire product lines and whole markets are now being created and destroyed overnight. In Accenture's ongoing research, we have already identified this type of disruption in more than 30 industry segments.

The upshot? A "big bang" of success for those who make the leap to this next level of value creation, and a disaster for incumbents, who swiftly become obsolete.

To survive—and even thrive—amid *big bang disruption*, companies must learn the new shape of new product diffusion and the four stages of this curve, one that loosely tracks the metaphor of the big bang theory of the universe. (See figure: "The Four Stages of Big Bang

Disruption.") They must also embrace the new rules of strategy and competition that follow:

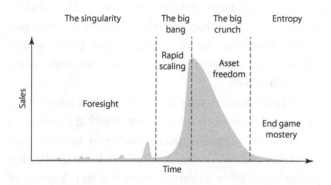

Note: The "shark fin" encapsulates the shift from business evolution driven by incremental technologies to big bang disruption powered by exponential technologies. Its strange shape reflects the new economics of information: the declining cost of innovation, the declining cost of information, and the declining cost of experimentation. Together, they have both shortened and skewed the life cycle of industry change, often to devastating effect.

Big bang disruption demands a new approach to strategy and planning, one that is different not in degree but in kind. The nature of your interactions with competitors, customers, suppliers, and other supply chain participants will be drastically altered. Every business function is affected—from research and development to manufacturing, marketing, sales, and even service. Your survival depends on new leadership and new ways of thinking.

The singularity: Find a truth teller

Big bang disruption happens in large part because experimentation has become both low cost and low risk, increasingly by using a wide range of new, often off-the-shelf component technologies. Many, many failures are likely before the right combination is found and proven to be cost-effective.

For incumbents, the failed early experiments send false signals, lulling executives into the misdirected belief that the disrupters are not ready for prime time. Enter the *truth tellers*—named for the characters on soap operas who move the plot forward by revealing big secrets. These are industry experts with profound insights into new technologies and customer behaviors, who can predict earlier than anyone else when small tremors signal imminent earthquakes.

One example is the North American executive of a Japanese carmaker who drove the company's decision to launch a luxury version of its popular SUV, based on his insight into fundamental shifts in income and spending in the US market. Only when he threatened to resign could he get the company to buy into his vision. His truth telling played an essential role in the carmaker's ongoing operations at the time.

Truth tellers speak a strange language, one that isn't focused on incremental change and the next quarter's results. Learning to find them is hard. Learning to listen to them is even harder.

The big bang: Exploit near-perfect market information

A big bang disruption, once created, enters the mass market at ultrahigh speed. Instead of a predictable process of selling to discrete, sequential market segments, big bang disrupters need worry only about two main categories of users: what we call *trial users*, and everybody else. At this stage, the goal is selling to everyone else—and fast.

The sudden success of big bang disrupters is driven by easy access to market opinion, facts, and comparison data, which creates something ever closer to consensus market opinion. The availability of near-perfect market information means consumers make fewer mistakes. They don't buy a mediocre product simply because manufacturers invest in more advertising. They wait until the right version—smartphones, 3D televisions, electric cars, solar power—emerges. Almost-there versions don't sell poorly—they don't sell at all.

Maintaining an intimate connection to trial users—the co-developers and, thanks to crowdsourcing services such as Kickstarter, co-funders—is therefore critical. Take, for example, the *smarthome* initiative of consumer electronics company Belkin International. Known as WeMo, the smartphone and tablet application has been designed to enable users to create specific commands for the on/off switches of basic home functions and electronics, such as lights. The company solicits and publishes user ideas for commands on its website, and when commands become popular enough—such as "If the Weather Channel says the sun has set, then have WeMo switch on the lights"—Belkin integrates them into the app's default list of commands for *all* WeMo users.

The big crunch: Collar your risk

Some companies do survive the inevitable downturn—in many cases, emerging in the new version of the industry in a position of greater leverage and profitability. But how?

The first step requires tough-minded management, sufficiently steeped in big bang strategy. Assets must be shed, products must be retired, business models allowed to sunset. Incumbents must prepare for the immediate evacuation of current markets and be ready to liquidate once-strategic assets.

Only then can incumbents unlock the hidden value of core, often intangible, assets. Traditional accounting still leads management to concentrate on the value of hard assets rather than expertise, brands, patents, and human resources. But in a fight against big bang disruption, intangibles are often the most valuable assets incumbents have.

Industry leaders may have a hard time committing themselves fully to transformation, creating an opening for perennial second-banana incumbents to shed their assets first and take their expertise, brand, and intellectual property into other industries where change is happening at a slower pace. When the film-based photo industry collapsed, it was Fujifilm and not Kodak that survived.

Entropy: Ride off into the sunset

In entropy, the big bang process comes full circle. The old industry is dead, and a new one has risen from the ashes. The new industry now waits for pressure to build and technology to advance through a new generation of failed market experiments, signaling the start of the next shift.

Companies must look closely at the phenomenon of industry sunset. How do assets get liquidated? How do old technologies and the facilities needed to manufacture and distribute them get recycled or retired? What financial tools are available to smooth the transition, even for industries that are "too big to fail"?

In this new diversification, the successful launch of a big bang disruption only buys you a license to try again. And your own success becomes your biggest competitive threat. Serial big bang disrupters effectively put themselves out of business first, before the competition, emerging as new enterprises that share the same name but often little else. Successful brand associations and truth-teller networks may be their most valuable assets.

Like Fujifilm, companies must imagine new uses in new industries for their products and, most importantly, capabilities. And, as Amazon has done, incumbents in this stage should imagine their business as a platform that provides value for a wide range of other businesses in many industries.

These ideas only begin to touch on the details of strategy and risk management in each of the four phases. Executives must ascertain the movement of disrupters in their own industries, and begin to put in place the capabilities necessary for success in a world that doesn't play by the old rules of business.

Business managers should heed the tacit warning given by a character in Hemingway's novel *The Sun Also Rises*, about the ways businesses fail. When asked how he went bankrupt, he replies, "Two ways. Gradually and then suddenly."

NATHAN FURR
From capturing to creating value

Nathan Furr (United States) is a professor of strategy and innovation at INSEAD in Paris and a recognized expert in the fields of innovation and technology strategy. He has multiple books and articles published by outlets such as *Harvard Business Review* and *MIT Sloan Management Review*, including his bestselling book *The Innovator's Method*.

Lean Startup has helped entrepreneurs, designers, and software developers manage uncertainty, but many managers and leaders struggle to apply these tools within their organizations, as they often run counter to traditional managerial thinking and practice. How do you suggest to solve this?

If we are honest, the real issue isn't the difficulty of adopting Lean Startup.

Lean Startup is just one of several emerging methodologies (e.g., design thinking, agile methodology) that provide valuable tools to navigate the uncertainty of innovation.

The real issue is how to manage uncertainty, which is something very difficult for traditional management. Why? Because traditional management was designed to solve a different problem. Traditional management was developed in response to the coordination problems created by the emergence of large firms during the Industrial Revolution. Thus traditional management was developed to help managers capture value—to execute, optimize, and coordinate. It wasn't developed to help managers create value—to discover, explore, and pivot.

Lean Startup represents one of many tools we are finding we need in this era of uncertainty to lead a more agile organization. This doesn't invalidate the value of our existing management knowledge, but it does mean we need new tools to complement our existing traditional management tools if big companies are going to survive in an environment of increasing uncertainty.

To follow up on this, you talk about the Innovator's Method. What is that?

I believe that Lean Startup, design thinking, agile methodologies, business model innovation, open innovation, and ideation are all related tools to manage the uncertainty of innovation.

Like the proverb of the blind men feeling and describing different parts of the same elephant, these frameworks each provide unique insights into the innovation process, but they ultimately describe the same underlying thing—the innovation process. The Innovator's Method is a synthesis of these many frameworks and insights from our research about how to apply these tools in established companies.

Can you give some examples of these tools being applied in established companies?

First, we observed that many companies start with a single methodology (e.g., design thinking, agile methodology, or Lean Startup) and then eventually integrate two or more frameworks to create what is essentially the Innovator's Method.

Our hope is that the book provides these firms a shortcut. But we have seen the ideas applied by many companies beyond more well-known examples (e.g., Amazon and Google), including Intuit, General Electric, Unilever, Philips, Cisco, United Technologies Corporation, and more recently, companies like Telenor and Solvay.

These methods are used for individual innovation projects (e.g., Cisco's CHILL-X spinning out healthcare and supply chain startups) as well as transforming the company to become more agile (e.g., Telenor, General Electric, United Technologies Corporation).

You mention the Cisco CHILL-X, which is a very interesting concept, I think.

To those who don't know about Cisco's "innovation machine," they have, among other things, their Cisco Hyper-Innovation Living Labs (CHILL). True to its name, CHILL provokes disruption by emulsifying solutions from noncompeting companies in various industries. This involves mustering senior executives from Fortune 500 companies at undisclosed locations around the globe for 48 hours. The locations of these conclaves are trivial; it's the ideas and solutions that are most intriguing.

Of course, a big part of this lies in the leadership. So how does a leader support innovation in the best possible way?

Most leaders feel a great deal of responsibility as the chief decision-makers to lead the way into the future, but I would encourage leaders to see themselves instead as the chief experimenter. When you face uncertainty, rather than trying to be the next Steve Jobs and hope you can correctly guess the future, I encourage leaders to empower junior people to run the rapid experiments that will reveal the future. This involves helping to frame the experiment, liberate the resources, and then constructively push people to create the future with you.

So let us talk a bit more about CHILL and Lean Startup. CHILL is a boot camp for innovation. The Minimum Viable Products (MVPs) are raw prototypes born from sheer brute force. This makes sense, because Lean Startup is designed around the idea of uncertainty. However, don't we actually know quite a lot about the future, if we just manage to distinguish between hard and soft trends and understand the new technologies shaping our world?

I'm not sure we know what the future will be. I think we all know things are changing quickly, but where it will end up we may not understand well enough. We may never understand it until we arrive.

I believe we could learn something important from physics. Physics is the most tangible of all the sciences yet the only science with an uncertainty principle. In essence, the uncertainty principle underscores that there is fundamental uncertainty in the universe that no amount of measurement precision can resolve (i.e., the uncertainty principle argues the more precisely we try to measure one value, such as speed, the less well we understand its paired value, such as position). I think the same could be said of our macro future—we know things are moving fast, but the faster it moves, the less well we understand where it will end up.

What do we do tomorrow? Instead of the more general advice, what should the reader of this book do tomorrow? A five- or ten-step plan—as concrete as possible.
In the Innovator's Method we lay out a four-element plan about what to do to generate ideas and turn them into new businesses.

More generally, I believe that in a world of uncertainty, taking action is the most powerful tool we have. One of my co-authors, Kate O'Keeffe, likes to say that she spent the first half of her career obsessed with finding the measures that could identify an innovation success early on. Ultimately, she gave up and argued, "Just start doing stuff." I do believe there is magic in action. It reveals the uncertain landscape. So, beyond the book, I would simply say, Start today.

PERFECTIONISM IS A DISEASE.
PROCRASTINATION IS A DISEASE.
ACTION IS THE CURE.

Richie Norton

SIMON SINEK
Innovation is born from the struggle

Simon Sinek is leading a movement to inspire people to do the things that inspire them. He is a trained ethnographer and author of *Start with Why: How Great Leaders Inspire Everyone to Take Action*. Sinek is best known for discovering the Golden Circle and popularizing the concept of Why, the purpose, cause, or belief that drives every one of us.

In 1975, a young director with no big films credits under his belt set out to make a horror film. Steven Spielberg wanted his film filled with violent and gory shark attacks. He wanted us to watch as this massive animal, built to kill, would attack his unsuspecting prey. But there was a problem. The mechanical sharks that were supposed play a staring role in the film rarely worked as expected. As much as the young director wanted graphic shark attacks, he couldn't have them.

Frustrated, the team found another solution. They left most of the violence to our imaginations. Viewers would see a fin, then someone would disappear under the water, and then the water would turn red. That's it.

In other scenes, we wouldn't even see a fin, we'd see a yellow barrel surfing across the water, knowing that it was a shark, deep below, towing the rope attached to the barrel toward the next victim. The effect was so scary and so powerful it influenced our entire society.

Though people were of course aware of sharks prior, there was little thought given to them when they went to the beach. After *Jaws*, however, there was a significant increase in shark hysteria that remains to this day. The funny thing is that more people are killed by dogs each year than have been killed by sharks since they started counting shark attacks.

The brilliant way in which Spielberg told the story of *Jaws* did not happen in a brainstorming session and it was certainly not planned. It was the solution he found when what he wanted wasn't possible. The malfunctioning robots forced him to find another solution.

We have a false belief that innovation happens with lots of money and resources. In fact, the opposite is true. Only through a lack of resources, a lack of money, or something going wrong are we able to truly innovate—to truly reimagine how something could work. This is why large companies rarely produce truly innovative products—because they have the money and resources to build anything they want. The problem is, the things they want aren't that innovative because they weren't hindered or forced to find new ways. Small businesses, in comparison, are where big ideas happen. Slim on money and resources, they figure out how to make something work with what they have. Then big businesses buy the small businesses for their big ideas.

To be clear, Spielberg was also a student of film. Without his mechanical shark, he was able to defer to his knowledge. He knew the techniques that Alfred Hitchcock used in his movies to build suspense—foreboding music, simple details, and an view of the aftermath. The suspense, Spielberg knew, happened in our imaginations, not in our eyes. Though he knew this, he didn't need to tap that knowledge until he had to. And that's where having less produces more. There are plenty of smart people at large companies who don't tap their brilliance because they don't need to. They have all the resources they need. Smart entrepreneurs, in contrast, have no choice but to rely on their smarts, and that's why they can run innovation circles around large companies every single day.

Innovation is not born from the dream; innovation is born from the struggle. Innovation, at its core, is not simply about building the future; innovation is about solving problems in the present. And the best innovations, just like the shark in *Jaws*, is often something we don't even know is there.

Note: This article was originally published on Simon's blog.

SETH GODIN
You don't need more time

Seth Godin (United States) is the author of 18 books that have been bestsellers around the world and have been translated into more than 35 languages. He writes about the postindustrial revolution, the way ideas spread, marketing, quitting, leadership, and most of all, changing everything. Before his work as a writer and a blogger, Godin was vice president of direct marketing at Yahoo!

As organizations and individuals succeed, it gets more difficult to innovate. There are issues of coordination, sure, but mostly it's about fear. The fear of failing is greater, because it seems as though you've got more to lose.

So urgency disappears first. Why ship it today if you can ship it next week instead? There are a myriad of excuses, but ultimately it comes down to this: if every innovation is likely to fail, or at the very least, be criticized, why be in such a hurry? Go to some more meetings, socialize it, polish it, and then, one day, you can ship it.

Part of the loss of urgency comes from a desire to avoid accountability. Many meetings are events in which an organization sits in a room until someone finally says, "Okay, I'll take responsibility for this." If you're willing to own it, do you actually need a meeting, or can you just email a question or two to the people you need information from?

Thus, we see the two symptoms of the organization unable to move forward with alacrity, the two warning signs of the person in the grip of the resistance: "I can take my time, and if I'm lucky, I can get you to wonder who to blame."

You don't need more time, you just need to decide.

Read the history of the original Mac and you'll be amazed at just how fast it got done. Willie Nelson wrote three hit songs in one day. To save the first brand I was responsible for, I redesigned five products in less than a day. It takes a team of six at Lays potato chips a year to do one.

The urgent dynamic is to ask for signoffs and to push forward, relentlessly. The accountable mantra is "I've got this." You can feel this happening when you're around it. It's a special sort of teamwork, a confident desperation. Not the desperation of hopelessness but the desperate effort that comes from being hopeful.

THE CHALLENGE, IT TURNS OUT,
ISN'T IN PERFECTING YOUR
ABILITY TO KNOW WHEN TO
START AND WHEN TO STAND BY.
THE CHALLENGE IS GETTING INTO
THE HABIT OF STARTING.

Seth Godin

TIM VANG
Pretotype or die

Tim Vang (Denmark) is co-founder and CEO of preeto. He is the quintessence of innovation, experimentation, and entrepreneurship with 20+ years of experience from the start-up sphere. Now focusing on bringing the entrepreneurial spirit into the corporate world around the globe, Tim pioneered crowdfunding in 2004.

Exponential growth has made its way into numerous industries. The development of epoch-making products and services is fed daily by new technology, and large businesses are suddenly overtaken on the inside track by intelligent and agile startups that understand how to exploit technology to its fullest. Well-established businesses must increasingly close. And this is only the tentative beginning of the exponential growth!

With the same starting point, Google used a couple of years to develop *pretotyping*—a powerful tool that immediately enables businesses to be able, quickly and cheaply, to test the market in a world characterized by fierce competition, critical consumers, much shorter product life cycles, and technological exponential growth. Pretotyping is a vital tool in the new reality and addresses both entrepreneurs and corporates that don't want to be overtaken by two people in a garage.

Time to change direction

Despite a flood of books and articles on innovation, business development, and the like, incredibly little has happened in these fields. Even large international players are whip shy about acting on the opportunities taking place outside their front doors, where the great majority of all businesses still use outdated methods for development of new products and services. Traditional tools such as market analyses, trend studies, and business plans all have one thing in common: they build on well-meaning assumptions of what they think customers want. Decisions must be based on market data and not based on customers' opinions gathered via interviews, focus groups, or the business's own beliefs about their customers' needs.

Selling the skin before the bear is shot

Most of you probably know about *proto*typing, which contributes to forming an idea or a concept on the path to a more or less functioning product or service (editor's note: the term *product* is used herein). Prototyping answers the question of whether a product in reality can be created using the available technology and knowledge or whether a design is satisfactory. But why use resources to build something that the market isn't interested in or ready for, despite what the price, target group, and market analyses have all indicated? Even projects executed in world-class circumstances fail in a frightening 80% of cases when they're launched on the market, simply because they were based on the wrong premises.

What would it mean for your company if you knew that you were having the right product before you made it? *Preto*typing distinguishes quite clearly between a good idea and a good business idea. The decisive aspect is getting the most valid market data with the smallest possible use of resources. It is all about testing assumptions on market terms and verifying positively or negatively whether a given product has the potential for commercial success. Pretotyping has just one purpose: to find out whether customers are willing to buy a product or start using it here and now. In other words, small experiments before large investments.

Failing cheaply

When Sara Blakely, entrepreneur, founder of Spanx, and self-made billionaire, relates her success story, her speech of thanks is always directed at her father. Every day during her childhood, he never asked Sara how her day had been. Instead, he asked her what she'd failed at that day. Sara was brought up in a culture of errors, which put her in a position to challenge the status quo and test new limits and learn from her mistakes. By comparison, many organizations suffer from a zero-error culture (although something else may be stated in the business's values and mission statement). If you take large chances and fail, you'll get a warning or, in the worst case, you'll be fired. But if, on the other hand, the business is successful, you'll be rewarded on the condition that you did everything correctly.

Pretotyping makes it possible to take big chances with little risk by doing things in a completely new way. That gives the business the possibility of failing easily and cheaply four times in a row, for example, and still hitting the jackpot the next time. With pretotyping, your failures cost you next to nothing; in return, the gains can be larger than one can imagine at first glance because you can test breakthrough ideas.

A real startup mindset

Pretotyping is more than a tool; it's a mindset. Pretotyping gives businesses wider wings with which to rise to new heights and allows them to ride on a wave of products that have the potential for exponential growth. That makes the business capable of competing with agile startups, which are capturing the arena with increasing speed. No dearly bought campaign or hype can sell a product that from the get-go doesn't match the customers' demands. The rule that applies to every business is to start small and test the market before the big guns are deployed. In Silicon Valley, pretotyping has become an organic standard in startups but also in the giants. The point is that as a pretotyper you understand the value of speedy and almost resource-free iterations being tested on the real market, no matter how big an organization you are in.

Empty air

A pretotype is mainly made up of empty air—in a good way. Fundamentally, you're making people believe that a product or a service exists that isn't found in reality. It is from this that the term *pretotyping* derives—from *pretending*. This means that consumers are first told you're shooting with blanks when they have their money in their hands. You therefore pretotype most often with a selection of potential customers to learn about conversion rates and contexts with their next interaction. If a customer experiences that the product or service, which you pretend exists, is a test, then the pretotype hasn't been executed properly. This may sound a little bit like a magician and his tricks, but it is precisely what Alberto Savoia (when he was at Google) has used years on systematizing.

1-2-3 pretotype

Is pretotyping, then, just another theory from the 75,000-plus books on innovation, each requiring you read 350-odd pages and an appendix that's twice as long? *No!* The fact is that pretotyping is a true game-changer that businesses can start to use very quickly. It's also very easy to learn, as in just some hours you'll be armed to fight with methods such as Fake Door, Pinocchio, and One Night Stand. With pretotyping in your toolbox, you'll ensure that your organization can test physical products, technology, and services across consumer groups—cheaply, quickly, and efficiently. Make your business entrepreneurial with the emphasis on failing often, daring more, and not least taking healthy decisions based on data from the real world.

Pretotyping Manifesto

Innovators beat ideas.
Pretotypes beat product types.
Building beats talking.
Simplicity beats features.
Now beats later.
Commitment beats committees.
Data beats opinions.

Take risks,
Tim

MOST PROTOTYPES ARE BUILT
TO ANSWER QUESTIONS SUCH
AS "CAN WE BUILD IT?" OR "WILL
IT WORK AS EXPECTED?"
INSTEAD OF FOCUSING ON
QUESTIONS SUCH AS "SHOULD
WE BUILD IT AT ALL?" OR "IF WE
BUILD IT, WILL PEOPLE BUY IT
AND USE IT?"

Alberto Savoia

STEVE BLANK
Startups are not a smaller version of a large company

Steve Blank (United States) is a serial entrepreneur recognized for developing the Customer Development methodology, which launched the Lean Startup movement. Blank is also co-founder of E.piphany and has spent 30 years within the high-tech industry, founding or working within eight startup companies, four of which have gone public.

In the last few years, we've recognized that a startup is not a smaller version of a large company. We're now learning that companies are not larger versions of startups.

There's been lots written about how companies need to be more innovative, but very little on what stops them from doing so.

Companies looking to be innovative face a conundrum: every policy and procedure that makes them efficient execution machines stifles innovation.

Facing continuous disruption from globalization, China, the internet, the diminished power of brands, changing workforces, and so on, existing enterprises are establishing corporate innovation groups. These groups are adapting or adopting the practices of startups and accelerators—disruption and innovation rather than direct competition, customer development versus more product features, agility and speed versus lowest cost.

But paradoxically, in spite of all their seemingly endless resources, *innovation inside of an existing company is much harder* than inside a startup. For most companies,

it feels like innovation can only happen by exception and heroic efforts, not by design. The question is *why*.

The enterprise: Business model execution

We know that a startup is a temporary organization designed to *search* for a repeatable and scalable business model. The corollary for an enterprise is as follows:

A company is a permanent organization designed to execute a repeatable and scalable business model.

Once you understand that existing companies are designed to *execute*, then you can see why they have a hard time with continuous and disruptive innovation.

Every large company, whether it can articulate it or not, is executing a proven business model(s). A business model guides an organization to create and deliver products/service and make money from it. It describes the product/service, who it is for, what channel sells/

delivers it, how demand is created, how the company makes money, and so on.

Somewhere in the dim past of the company, it too was a startup *searching* for a business model. But now, as the business model is repeatable and scalable, most employees take the business model as a given, and instead focus on the *execution* of the model—what it is they are supposed to do every day when they come to work. They measure their success on metrics that reflect success in execution, and they reward it.

It's worth looking at the tools companies have to support successful execution and explain why these same execution policies and processes have become impediments and are antithetical to continuous innovation.

20th-century management tools for execution

In the 20th century, business schools and consulting firms developed an amazing management stack to assist companies to *execute*. These tools brought clarity to corporate strategy and product line extension strategies, and made product management a repeatable process. Some examples include the following:

- The Boston Consulting Group 2 × 2 growth share matrix: An easy-to-understand strategy tool—a market selection matrix for companies looking for growth opportunities
- Strategy maps: A visualization tool to translate strategy into specific actions and objectives, and to measure the progress of how the strategy gets implemented.
- Product management tools such as Stage-Gate®: The product management process assumes that the product/market fit is known, and the products

can get spec'd and then implemented in a linear fashion.
- Strategy becomes visible in a company when you draw the structure to execute the strategy. The most visible symbol of execution is the organization chart. It represents where employees fit in an execution hierarchy; showing command and control hierarchies—who's responsible, what they are responsible for, and who they manage below them and report to above them.

All these tools—strategy, product management, and organizational structures—have an underlying assumption that the business model—which features customers want, who the customers are, what channel sells/delivers the product or service, how demand is created, how the company makes money, and so on—is known, and that all the company needed is a systematic process for execution.

Driven by key performance indicators (KPIs) and processes

Once the business model is known, the company organizes around that goal, measures efforts to reach the goal, and seeks the most efficient ways to do so. This systematic process of execution needs to be repeatable and scalable throughout a large organization by employees with a range of skills and competencies. Staff functions in finance, human resources, legal departments, and business units develop KPIs, processes, procedures, and goals to measure, control, and execute.

Paradoxically, these very KPIs and processes that make companies more efficient are the root causes of corporations' inability to be agile, responsive innovators.

This is a big idea.

Finance: The goals for public companies are driven primarily by financial KPIs. They include return on net assets (RONA), return on capital deployed, internal rate of return (IRR), net/gross margins, earnings per share, marginal cost/revenue, debt/equity, EBIDA, price earning ratio, operating income, net revenue per employee, working capital, debt-to-equity ratio, acid test, accounts receivable/payable turnover, asset utilization, loan loss reserves, minimum acceptable rate of return, and so on.

(A consequence of using corporate finance metrics such as RONA and IRR is that it's a lot easier to get these numbers to look great by (1) outsourcing everything, (2) getting assets off the balance sheet, and (3) only investing in things that pay off fast. These metrics stack the deck against a company that wants to invest in long-term innovation.)

These financial performance indicators then drive the operating functions (sales, manufacturing, etc.) or business units that have their own execution KPIs (market share, quote-to-close ratio, sales per rep, customer acquisition/activation costs, average selling price, committed monthly recurring revenue, customer lifetime value, churn/retention, sales per square foot, inventory turns, etc.)

Corporate KPIs, policy, and procedures: Innovation killers

HR process: Historically, human resources was responsible for recruiting, retaining, and removing employees to execute known business functions with known job specs. One of the least obvious but most important HR processes, and ultimately the most contentious issue in corporate innovation, is the difference in *incentives.* The incentive system for a company focused on execution is driven by the goal of meeting and exceeding "the

(quarterly/yearly) plan." Sales teams are commission based; executive compensation is based on EPS, revenue, and margin; business units are based on revenue, margin contribution, and so on.

What does this mean?

Every time another execution process is added, corporate innovation dies a little more.

The conundrum is that every policy and procedure that makes a company an efficient execution machine stifles innovation.

Innovation is chaotic, messy, and uncertain. It needs radically different tools for measurement and control. It needs the tools and processes pioneered in lean startups.

While companies intellectually understand innovation, they don't really know how to build innovation into their culture or how to measure its progress.

What to do?

It may be that the current attempts to build corporate innovation are starting at the wrong end of the problem. While it's fashionable to build corporate incubators, there's little evidence that they deliver more than "innovation theater," because internal culture applies execution measures/performance indicators to the output of these incubators and allocates resources to them same way as to executing parts of company.

Corporations that want to build continuous innovation must realize that *innovation happens not by exception but as integral to all parts of the corporation.*

To do so, they will realize that a company needs *innovation* KPIs, policies, processes, and incentives. (Our *investment readiness level* is just one of those metrics.)

These enable innovation to occur as an integral and parallel process to execution—by design not by exception.

Lessons learned

- Innovation inside of an existing company is *much* harder than a startup.
- KPIs and processes are the root cause of corporations' inability to be agile and responsive innovators.
- Every time another execution process is added, corporate innovation dies a little more.
- Intellectually, companies understand innovation, but they don't have the tools to put it into practice.
- Companies need different policies, procedures, and incentives designed for innovation.
- Currently, the data we use for execution models the past.
- Innovation metrics need to be predictive for the future.
- These tools and practices are coming…

More great blogs by Steve Blank at www.steveblank.com

THOMAS WEDELL-WEDELLSBORG
When *not* to trust your gut

Thomas Wedell-Wedellsborg (Denmark) is a researcher, public speaker, and co-author of *Innovation as Usual*, published by Harvard Business Review Press. He speaks at events around the world and has been named as one of the world's 20 most influential thinkers. He can be followed at www.wedellsblog.com.

Several years ago, as I was finishing a 2-year MBA degree, I decided to start my own company. The idea was simple: create a private online community for the alumni of the world's top-tier business schools. The idea was inspired by the social network ASmallWorld, which had great success then.

At the time, I had a couple of months left of my MBA, so when one of my professors offered a course in entrepreneurship, I enrolled immediately. Thus, just prior to launching my startup, I received a thorough education in all the mistakes that startup founders typically make.

And then—to my great retrospective horror—I went out and *made* many of those mistakes. And they weren't only trifles. In short, my bad decisions ended up killing my startup.

A special kind of idiot?

The fate of my startup triggered a round of deep introspection. I've always regarded myself as a reasonably intelligent person, and I have gradually built up a CV that points in the same direction: I've published a book at Harvard, and companies around the world now hire me to give talks to their leaders. But the failure of my startup was an unpleasantly concrete testimony that I was perhaps not quite as smart as I thought. It is one thing to make mistakes as you try to build a company, but you have to be a special kind of idiot to make mistakes *that you already know are typical startup mistakes*. Right?

I share this story because it offers a crucial piece of advice for being successful with innovation, whether in a startup or elsewhere. In the period that followed, I began to understand what had gone wrong. On the surface, my mistakes were varied: I chose the wrong business partners, I made the website far too complex, and I used far too much energy on our competitors. But there was a common denominator to all these things: the role of my intuition.

Death by feature creep

Take, for example, the decision about how many features the first version of my website should have. I knew very well that it was essential to get a "bare bones" prototype out into the real world as fast as possible. I also knew that founders systematically underestimate how much time it takes to build something. But the idea of launching a half-finished site felt *so* wrong—so much against my gut feeling—that I didn't do it, but instead chose to put a load of features on the site. As a result, launching the site took a fatally long time.

The pattern was the same in my other mistakes: I relied too much on my intuition. And that applied especially in the situations where my intuition felt *strong*—that is, where I had a very clear sense that I was right. In those situations, I often chose to follow my gut feeling, although both my advisers and the startup literature unambiguously pointed in another direction.

Big mistake. The truth is both simple and uncomfortable: *The strength of your gut feeling has nothing to do with whether your gut feeling is right.*

Three steps to a better gut feeling

The ability to use your intuition selectively is in my view the most important discipline that you must master to succeed with innovation. This is the case because there is currently a great deal of good advice available out there about how to build something new—including the advice in the book you're holding now. But none of that advice is of any use if you don't have the ability to recognize when your intuition may err—and the discipline to follow up on that recognition in your actions, even if it feels wrong. In the following, I share three pieces of advice that can help you in this process.

1. Understand the limitations

Firstly, it is necessary to realize when you *shouldn't* trust your intuition. This is a subject that researchers such as Robin Hogarth and Daniel Kahneman have studied for years, and their research has offered a clear rule of thumb: Your intuition is reliable if and only if the decision is of a type that you've made *many times*, and if you've got *clear feedback* on those decisions.

Golfers who train their putting game get clear and immediate feedback on every stroke, and after hundreds of strokes, they develop a good intuition for reading the course's slope and distance correctly. Interviewing job candidates, on the other hand, is an area where the research shows that you should not trust your intuition about a candidate. Most people do not recruit very many applicants, and, as a rule, the feedback on a recruitment decision is both delayed and complicated by a large number of other factors—which means that your intuition doesn't get trained properly. And indeed, the research shows that interviewers who rely heavily on their intuition systematically make poorer recruitment decisions.

The next time you're about to make a big decision, ask yourself: Have I made this type of decision many times before? And have I gotten good feedback on my choices? If the answer to one of these questions is no, you should be wary about listening to your gut feeling—even if it feels strong and right.

2. Create a framework for the important decisions

A second good principle is to create a framework for decisions that you (or your staff) often make. In my book *Innovation as Usual*, I talk about creating an *architecture* for your decisions—that is, establishing structures and processes that help you avoid systematic errors.

An interesting example is found in Prehype, a New York–based venture development company that builds startups together with large businesses, and on which I recently published a case study (*Startup as a Service: The Prehype Model*, IESE Publishing, February 2016).

When working with their clients to build products and services, Prehype constantly runs into the problem that I experienced myself: *feature creep*, or the temptation to add far too many features to a product. To avoid this,

Prehype has institutionalized a simple rule: if it will take more than 100 days to launch the first prototype, then the idea is too complex. As I relate in the case study, this 100-day rule and similar principles have made it possible for Prehype to build a number of successful ventures in a very short time without falling into the perfectionist trap that killed my own startup.

3. Accept that it feels wrong

The last principle has to do with managing your emotions. People often say that you should be ready to "step out of your comfort zone" when you work with innovation—and that sounds reasonable enough. But in my experience, that mildly anodyne expression doesn't really capture *how* horribly, gut-churningly wrong it feels to go against your intuition. I'm a perfectionist by nature, and if I so much as think about launching something half-finished, it's as if my whole being rises up in protest.

It's a very strong feeling, and it's difficult to ignore. But that is nevertheless precisely what you should prepare to do once in a while if you are in the business of creating something new. Accept that the road to success will sometimes require you to make decisions that feel wrong—and then try to find small, simple ways of testing your intuition, so it will be trained to understand that it's not always right. Your gut feeling *is* useful, but it's not a perfect tool—and you can quickly get into trouble if you don't learn to take its limitations into account. I learned the hard way. Don't follow my example.

CREATIVE MINDS DON'T FOLLOW RULES, THEY FOLLOW WILL.

Amit Kalantri

JACOB DE GEER
Banking is essential, but banks are not

Jacob de Geer (Sweden) is a serial entrepreneur and co-founder and CEO of iZettle, one of Europe's fastest-growing companies. Based in Stockholm, the financial technology company revolutionized mobile payments in 2011 with the world's first mini chip card reader and software for mobile devices. Today, iZettle is a one-stop shop for commerce for small businesses around the world, and hundreds of thousands are using iZettle's tools to take payments, to register and track sales, and to get funding.

You've said that your goal is to democratize commerce around the world. What do you mean by that?

I know that *democratizing* is a very big word, but it works well to explain our mission. When we started iZettle, there wasn't a viable option that helped Europe's 20 million small businesses take card payments. There were expensive and complicated options for bigger companies but nothing for people selling stuff at a flea market or in a small café. It was clear what we needed to do: help them to accept payments just as easily as big corporations. Simply put, we wanted to democratize payments.

So, to make a long struggle short, we developed a mini chip card reader and a point-of-sale app that basically turns smartphones into cash registers. But what we really brought to market was the idea that small businesses should have the same opportunities as big businesses. We quickly learned that small business owners are underserved by the traditional finance industry in many other ways. So we branched out from our core mobile payments offering—adding services such as invoicing, business management, customer engagement, and more. That's why today we talk about democratizing commerce.

That sounds like a typical case for disruptive innovation—start with the customers that no one is currently serving?

Yes, and there are still many millions of small businesses being underserved by old-school financial players. Thanks to digitalization and high smartphone penetration, we can now give them access to the same tools the big players have. We compete in a highly regulated industry, and all of these rules and regulations were created much before smartphones and digital solutions. So, the biggest disruption for us was really the online onboarding and making it easy to become a customer for both business owners and their consumers.

Where Uber is fighting the landscape of regulations, you guys have decided not to. How come?

We chose to try and work together with the regulators and have had countless conversations with different authorities. Finally, they approved our product and solution, as we managed to explain the injustice with the current system, which really wasn't built for small businesses.

With that said, I think innovative technology is always challenging and changing the regulatory landscape. As the Swedish mega entrepreneur Jan Stenbeck famously said, "Politics may beat money, but technology always beats politics."

How did you become aware of this hole in the market?

The whole thing started with my ex-wife coming home one night very frustrated. She ran a sole-trading business, and she had been at one of these big trade fairs. However, she couldn't offer any form of credit card payment solution, and since 50% of the people wanting to buy something from her didn't carry any cash, she missed out on 50% of her business potential. I asked her why she didn't get a card terminal, and she said that she would love to, but the card provider asked her for a very large amount of money and a 24-month subscription clause. That just didn't seem right to me.

Since iZettle was founded, other companies have joined the mobile point-of-sale (mPOS) race in Europe. What's your vision of the current market and of your competition both in Europe and South America?

Many people make the mistake of thinking of us as solely a mobile payments solution provider, but today we compete in many different market segments. Our role is essentially to level the playing field for merchants and help them sell more. At the same time, we want to simplify things for them and help them work smarter, so that their daily accounting is done with the press of a button. This saves them expensive accountants and complex business commerce solutions.

If you don't compete with mobile payment solutions, where is the benchmark for iZettle?

Well, we're creating a new category so there's not one benchmark but several. Focus for us moving forward will be leveraging the data we have, and scale with the help of artificial intelligence and machine learning. The last five years we've been at the center of an ecosystem which every day provides us with 200 million data points. By making use of the data gathered, we're able to design products custom made for the needs of small businesses. As an example, we're now able to offer merchants a cash advance. Instead of relying on credit ratings, we track your daily sales data and can pretty accurately estimate what your sales will look like in the future. This enables us to offer merchants quick and easy access to capital, which helps them expand their business.

So you basically tell the merchants to stop going to the local bank for a business loan and instead getting the credit from you guys?

The bank will think of these small companies as a high-risk segment. Therefore, they will either say no or give them a very poor deal. While banks read yesterday's news, we look at real-time data and can offer eligible merchants a tailor-made financing service. Repayments are automatic and tied to card sales, so when business is booming, you pay more, and when things are slow, you pay less.

You have a Swedish background just like the founders of Spotify and Skype. What is up with you Swedish people and tech startups?

When it comes to hosting unicorns, Stockholm is second only to Silicon Valley. Just like Björn Borg inspired generations of Swedish tennis players, startups like Spotify and Skype have inspired a new generation of startups. We now have a thriving ecosystem, with second and third generation entrepreneurs supporting new wave of entrepreneurs.

How is the financial industry going to be disrupted in the future? What do you think will happen?

I think we'll continue to see fintechs accelerate their growth and grab market share from banks. Banks won't disappear any time soon as they continue to sit on critical infrastructure and have lots of cash, but they will have to start thinking seriously about their next step and what they can do to remain relevant. They basically have to make a choice: either fight for the customer relationship, leverage their data, and deliver a superior experience and price or take a step back, become a platform for fintechs to build on, and let fintechs do what they do best: face the consumer.

Right now, disruption is happening in so many places. There is no big bang. It's an ongoing process built on trial and error, and all the areas within the financial industry will be under fire. I think that what we'll see is a redistribution of revenues and profits rather than a closure of the major banks. To quote Bill Gates, "Banking is essential. Banks are not."

WE'RE TALKING ABOUT PAYMENTS, CUSTOMERS CARE ABOUT SHOPPING.

Ranjit Sarai

SONIA ARRISON
Our hearts and minds will have much more time

Sonia Arrison (United States) is an author and policy analyst who has studied the impact of new technologies on society for the better part of a decade. She is a frequent media contributor and guest, and her work has appeared in many publications, including *CBS MarketWatch*, CNN, *The New York Times*, *The Wall Street Journal*, and *USA Today*. She is the author the national bestseller *100 Plus*.

Imagine having been married for 125 years. You are 150 years old, and your youngest child has just turned 110. You're happy and healthy. Life is good, and even though the clock is still ticking, you have much more time left than today. No reason to worry or even panic about death yet.

This might sound like science fiction to some, but to Sonia Arrison—bestselling author, analyst, and board member at the Thiel Foundation—this is not a futurist mirage. This is going to happen—rather sooner than later.

I had the pleasure of interviewing Sonia about the impact of technology on human life and innovation, and my first question to her was…

How will technology improve our health and impact the health sector in the future?

In the future, it will be completely natural to live much longer than today. We will also live a more healthy life, and even though we might be thinking less about death than we do now, we will continue to live meaningful lives, motivated by forces such as creativity, love, and honor.

When you look at the radical innovations going on in both labs and in clinical trials, everything is happening so fast. In the relatively near future, deaths from diseases like cancer and heart disease will be much lower, and we will live considerably longer and healthier.

One of the things impacting the health sector and our health as individuals is going to be artificial intelligence (AI). As we speak, AI is beginning to outperform doctors in areas such as radiology and predicting the onset of medically significant events such as heart attacks. It's pretty incredible.

So AI is going to play a vital role in the future. What about the field of regenerative medicine?

Regenerative medicine opens up the possibility of repairing people rather than just keeping them alive and sick.

This will drastically reduce our medical expenses and leave room for investing in other parts of our society.

When technology is going to play a huge part for humans, will it also make us feel less human? For example, I read about a neuroscientist at the University of Southern California in Los Angeles who has proposed that brain implants might be used to store and retrieve memories. His prosthesis would be intended to help those whose brains cannot form long-term memories because they are damaged.
Actually, I don't think that this kind of technology will make us feel less human.

I still feel human even though I Google things. I also feel human even though I might need a hearing aid—or glasses for that matter. Vaccines are another example of us influencing the human body with technology, but in these cases, it doesn't impact our feelings of being human. So my initial answer is no, but of course you never know until you get there.

Let us imagine that we have cured aging. It doesn't sound that futuristic anymore. If we live forever, or at least don't die due to aging, do we then still need God?
Well—some would argue that God gave us a brain. Perhaps we're using the tools that he gave us to improve our lives.

Whether or not we need God… I don't think it has much to do with aging in the sense of life and death, to be quite honest. If you study religion, you will see that it is mostly about life, not about death. Religion is concerned with how to live a good life. Religion is a way of seeking guidance for your life. So, the longer you live, the more guidance you might need, and the more religion might actually play a role.

It appears that humans are wired for spirituality, so I don't think that religion will ever really disappear from our lives. We're just entering a future where our hearts and our minds will get more time. Literally speaking.

Our hearts and minds will have much more time. That sounds nice, doesn't it?
Absolutely. Increasing health spans will give you much more time to reeducate yourself, dream, and innovate. Go on more holidays. Spend more time with people that you love. Have people around you longer.

You see no problems in this?
Every new development has its problems, but it's hard to precisely predict them and how they're going to show themselves.

What about this imaginary problem— namely, a company where some staff members are 150 years old and others are 25. How do we deal with this massive age and generation gap?
On the one hand, companies of the future will benefit from experienced staff members, but on the other hand, you're right that tensions might arise. Think about it: does a person who is 100 years old share meaningful cultural stories with someone that is 30? It's hard to say how

it will play out. If we are fortunate, we will be around to participate in the debate.

We have established that technology will impact our aging, our health, and our organizational environments. What about the impact on innovation in general?

I think it will be very positive and interesting! Studies show that innovation peaks much later in life than most people think. We're so used to hearing the Silicon Valley "young entrepreneur" story featuring people like Mark Zuckerberg and Steve Jobs, but it turns out that innovation typically peaks around the age of 40. One of the reasons for this peak is that at 40 we're still healthy, yet we have also had quite a lot of time to get educated and look at things in many different fields. This enables us to start making connections between different areas, which generates novel ideas. As we get older, we become better at connecting the dots.

However, shortly after the peak age, our innovation abilities start to decline again—likely due to health issues as people age. So, if people could be healthier for a longer period of time, it would also mean that innovation would continue at peak pace for more years of our lives.

It sounds like the brain could become the tech market of the future.

Absolutely. We already see edtech exploding, and educational services are all about our brain and different ways to strengthen it.

Virtual reality, augmentation, and AI are other examples of the importance of the brain for future innovation and business. For instance, Elon Musk has repeatedly made the argument that in the future we will need brain implants to stay relevant in a world that, he believes, will soon be dominated by AI. Proposing the artificial augmentation of human intelligence as a response to a boom in AI may seem a bit much, but it underscores the role of the brain as the tech market of the future.

Are there any ethical dilemmas in this as far as you are concerned? Are there examples where creativity becomes too creative?

Of course, and we will have discussions about this now and in the future. We already have, when it comes to genetics.

When it comes to different vocations and markets, we should accept the concept of *creative destruction*. This basically means that it's not always a bad thing when old ways of doing things fail and therefore die. If a business isn't fulfilling a need, and people don't value it anymore, it's okay that it dies.

For example, I like newspapers, and I'm willing to pay for the news, but I also accept that industries like the media need to be shaken up on a regular basis. Napster did the same to the music industry, and it still hasn't settled completely.

With the human brain and body, of course, this is an even more delicate area, and there will be moral dilemmas that require serious and careful thought. In Silicon Valley, where I live, we have dreamers and doers, and often they're combined. This has led to the saying "If you can dream it, you can do it." The obvious additional question is of course "You can do it, but should you do it?"

WE SHOULD TAKE CARE NOT TO MAKE THE INTELLECT OUR GOD; IT HAS, OF COURSE, POWERFUL MUSCLES, BUT NO PERSONALITY.

Albert Einstein

JIMMY MAYMANN
Disruption is something you must experience yourself

Jimmy Maymann (Denmark) is an award-winning entrepreneur and leader. He has founded a number of companies including GoViral, which he sold to AOL for more than $80 million. He is former CEO of *The Huffington Post*, former executive vice president at AOL Content and Consumer Brands, and is currently, among other things, chair of the United Nations project UNLive Online.

It was back in 2005 that I, the editor of this book, first heard about Jimmy Maymann, when he and some friends founded the company GoViral. At about the same time, my own startup began getting interested in video as a part of our communication, and the boys at GoViral went all out in precisely the field of video.

Before YouTube became really popular, Maymann and his co-founder Claus Moseholm began striving to make their vision grow large—by helping companies get their marketing messages out through viral, video-based marketing.

It was then that I talked with Jimmy for the first time, and I've followed his exciting career since from the sideline. After he and Moseholm made their large, three-digit-million exit from GoViral in 2012, Maymann was offered the top job at the internet media outlet *The Huffington Post*, which was quickly storming ahead, and he accepted.

Jimmy Maymann's job target was to double The *Huffington Post*'s 40 million monthly users within 2 years, but 3 years later, Jimmy had increased the number of users fivefold and had increased *The Huffington Post*'s presence from 2 to 14 markets. That echoed in the rest of the world, and in connection with a large round of acquisitions, Jimmy Maymann was given the responsibility for "consumer brands" at mass-media giant AOL.

When doing this interview, Jimmy was still CEO of The *Huffington Post*.

Jimmy, everybody's not only talking about innovation at the moment. The new buzzword is *disruption*. I'm currently attending an e-commerce conference with 1100 people, and this is no exception. How does disruption seem to you with your job and experience?

I think we must start by defining what it is we're talking about. In my view there's a considerable difference between digital transformation and disruption. In digital transformation, there are new technologies and a digitalization process that mean that many branches can and must develop. These open new possibilities for them but can also be an extension of and support for what we're already doing to some degree in business and innovation terms.

Disruption is quite different. It's completely new ways of acting or trading, such as the development of the sharing economy, which presuppose fundamentally new business models.

Unlike many competitors, you've experienced growth in the number of users and in your earnings. What have you done differently?

First and foremost, we've had a different culture than that of the traditional, older media groups.

On the one hand, we consider ourselves to be media, but we're more than that. We're a platform. Our approach is to use news to generate discussions and our community is very vital to us.

When we focus on some of the things that people are really interested in, then the involvement is 15 to 20 times larger than on The *New York Times*'s website, for example. We have more people sharing news and more who interact and debate.

When I came to *The Huffington Post*, the social media really started to play a very vital role for media such as us. Until I started there, we'd been world leaders in search engine optimization (SEO) and we'd ranked highly with our news in search results. We're still good at that type of thing, but now we focus just as hard on Facebook, Twitter, Instagram, and, soon, Snapchat.

We want to be world champion in understanding how people interact with news and with each other, and incisive in what is required for users to share the things we publish.

When you describe it like that, I can't help wondering whether you're actually delivering news. Aren't you really describing here how you became good at running and controlling online traffic?

Let me give you an example: One of our journalists writes a story of 1000 words. That takes her perhaps 3 hours. At some media groups, the journalist may retain a self-impression of writing *stories* but not *headlines*. That's not what it's like at *Huffington*.

At our media group, the journalist who writes the 1000-word story must also provide catchy headlines and find appropriate pictures. Our journalistic staff know that their news coverage is a matter of getting the message across to as many readers as possible.

It takes the journalist I mentioned 3 hours to write the story, no matter what, so why not see it as something quite natural that she should also contribute to getting people to actually interest themselves in the content?

But isn't it just clickbait that you're describing here? The media try to tempt the readers with headlines that may not represent the content, but get us to click on the page so they can earn money on their advertisements.

No. Fundamentally, this is about tomorrow's journalists, who in the future must be able to do more than write the basic story in an article. They must not sit back and say, "Journalists don't do that."

With regard to tempting people to click, we're very much aware of our responsibility. We reach over 200 million people, so we don't just put *anything* on the front page. You will often see a front page which also has stories that

don't spread much but on the basis of fundamental news criteria are important stories. That's why they're there.

The click part should also be understood as emphasizing that we're experts in data. We know that people say one thing but often do something else. We know precisely what they look at and click on, and therefore we have the in-house mantra "People come for the Kardashians, but stay for the Obamas."

Does that also mean that you recruit some other profiles than your competitors?

Yes, we do that to a great degree. Take, for example, us and The *Washington Post*. Our average age is 32 years. Theirs is somewhere in the 40s. Both The *Washington Post* and The *New York Times* have fantastic journalists, but they're not very open to change.

Our journalists are from the younger generation, and they've grown up with the new media. Thinking digitally is natural for them. For example, they understand that, when something happens here and now, we can make use of an authentic picture from a person actually "at the crime scene." The quality may not be quite as high as you'd normally expect of a photograph used in a newspaper, but it's important to get the story out. A traditional journalist or photographer would be against that attitude.

Are you in this way also calling on other businesses to take on younger people to a larger extent?

Without it sounding like age discrimination, yes. It is incumbent on us to create a mix—also in terms of age. I often see businesses that do not manage to get the new generation into central positions. That's something they *must* do.

As far as I'm concerned, I regularly ask young people from our teams to come in and tell me about a new technology that I may not really understand. I similarly often have exciting startups come past my office to pitch their new ideas and innovations to me.

You have to think in that way or else you miss out on a lot of the things that are taking place at the moment in the subcultures but which will very soon become mainstream.

Now you're part of a large organization. I'm thinking on behalf of small and medium-sized companies in particular. For them, the disruption challenge can seem really enormous. They don't have AOL's resources or your network, so what should they do with regard to the disruption agenda?

I come myself from the startup environment, so I know everything about lacking resources and lacking a network.

What is most decisive is that you get out and experience some of the many exciting new technologies yourself. You can't really understand 3D printing, virtual reality, or other phenomena if you haven't tried them. One thing is reading articles about them; it's something else to stand in the midst of it all.

For example, we're testing virtual reality right now at *The Huffington Post*. In the future, it can give us a completely unique opportunity for experiencing the stories and news. Instead of hearing abstractions about the Syrian refugee crisis, you can suddenly put VR equipment on and stand in the midst of it. Put yourself in the place of the narrator and feel the emotions and the people in a completely different way.

By trying out virtual reality yourself, it and other technologies that are growing by leaps and bounds become real in a completely different way, so you're better able to relate to them and see their potential—also for your own, smaller business.

So we must go out and try it, even if it seems scary?

Yes, but hopefully scary and exciting at the same time. We're facing a pronounced development on a par with the industrial revolutions that we've seen historically, but we're only at the beginning.

It will come, and it's coming in things like quantum computing, the internet of things, 3D printing, self-driving cars, and much more.

I believe that, as a business owner, you need to prioritize your time and get out and experience phenomena such as these yourself. Talk to the people who are building them right now and understand the possibilities they offer, rather than only looking at all the negative aspects. It's definitely worth the investment.

DANIEL BURRUS
How to anticipate the future

Daniel Burrus (United States) has built a worldwide reputation for predicting technological change and its impact on the world of business. He is the author of seven books, including *The New York Times* bestseller *Flash Foresight* and his new book *The Anticipatory Organization*, and is followed by millions of readers on social media. He is the founder of six companies; three were national leaders in the United States in their first year, and five were profitable within the first year of business.

The New York Times has referred to Daniel Burrus as one of the top three business gurus in the world, and he is a strategic advisor to executives from Fortune 500 companies, helping them to develop game-changing strategies based on his methodologies for capitalizing on technology innovations and their future impact.

I'm fascinated by Burrus's ability to accurately predict the future and not just guess. I'm also interested in his scientific approach to innovation and his methodologies on how to create business models and products that will actually work and succeed.

So, we met up and talked about the difference between hard and soft trends and Daniel's ideas on a different approach to how companies plan and innovate.

You teach what you consider to be the biggest missing competency in companies and organizations today: the ability to anticipate. Please tell me more about this.
We live in a world that reacts. The pace of change is increasing everywhere, and many think agility is the best way to deal with rapid change. I'm not saying that agility isn't good, because there are a lot of things that you can't accurately predict. There will always be changes that come out of nowhere. However, there are an amazing number of things we can accurately predict when we learn how to distinguish between what I call *hard trends*, trends that *will* happen, and *soft trends*, trends that *might* happen. Think of it as a two-sided coin. Agility is on one side, allowing you to react fast to unforeseen change, and the other side is anticipatory, allowing you to see what is coming and take action *before* the change occurs.

What do you think of agile innovation?

Agility is basically reacting quickly to change. Therefore, it's important to understand that agile innovation is reactive innovation. Agile innovation will keep you reacting to disruptive innovation created by others. For example, did Uber or Airbnb use agility to come up with their multibillion-dollar innovations? No, agility would not help them leap ahead with confidence. They identified the hard trends that were going to happen either through them or someone else, and took action with the confidence certainty can provide. The same hard-trend strategy is used by Amazon and Apple, giving them the ability to leap ahead with low risk and innovate quickly.

In the past few years, there have been several large organizations writing and teaching about the subject of exponential organizations and exponential growth, which is just as valuable as agile innovation is. But if you are going exponentially fast in the wrong direction, you will get into trouble exponentially faster.

Way back in 1983, I was the first to write and speak about the predictability and power of technology-driven exponential change, and that is indeed an important element to drive innovation and growth. But predictable exponential change is only about speed, not direction. When you learn to identify the hard trends that *will* have a massive impact, you can gain crucial insights for driving business innovation as well as disruption.

You're obviously right about that, but is that really something we can predict with a high level of certainty?

Absolutely! There is no shortage of trends out there. The problem is knowing which trends are going to happen and when. As I mentioned earlier, you can divide trends into two categories: hard trends and soft trends. Hard trends are based on future facts; they *will* happen. It's 100% certain. You can't stop them from happening, but you can see them ahead of time. The three main categories of hard trends are *technology, demographics*, and *government regulation*. The last one is usually a surprise, but equally surprising is how powerful this can be when you learn how to see the future of regulations and their related opportunities.

Using my hard-trend methodology, you can see disruptions, *before* they disrupt, and turn predictable disruption into an opportunity. You can see the problems you will have *before* you have them and pre-solve them. You can see the game-changers and take action on them *before* the game is changed on you.

What is a soft trend?

A soft trend *might* happen and is a trend that is based on an assumption, not future facts. There are various levels of assumptions with different levels of risk. The power of soft trends is that you can influence them to your advantage. In other words, if you don't like a soft trend, you can change it.

My hard-trend methodology is a proven methodology that represents a powerful way to manage risk. Strategies based on uncertainty have high risk; strategies based on certainty have low risk. When leaders understand the difference between the soft and hard trends, it allows them to both innovate and even disrupt with low risk.

Is there a way to know when a hard trend will happen?

Based on my research in 1983, when I started my company, I came across Moore's law, which basically states that processing power will double every 18 months as the price drops in half. Not a lot of people were looking at Moore's law in the early 1980s, but I knew he nailed it. Based on Moore's law, I identified what I called the Three Digital Accelerators: the predictable exponential growth of computing power, bandwidth, and digital storage. They don't follow the exact same exponential curves as Moore's law, but very close. Those are the three main factors driving the predictable and exponential pace of change. Hard trends provide the *what* and the Three Digital Accelerators provide the *when* to the visible future.

The key to harnessing the power of exponentiality is the ability to accurately anticipate the hard trends that are shaping the future.

I think that everybody wants to see the future, but can you tell me more about how you actually do it?

A key principle I teach is that if it can be done, it will be done, and if you don't do it, someone else will.

I've conducted over 35 years of research to understand trends and the driving forces of change. For example, in 1983, I listed digital electronics, distributed computing and the internet, optical storage, wireless networking, artificial intelligence, nanotech, supercomputers, genetic engineering—20 technology categories in all that would drive economic growth for decades to come. My original list of 20 has stood the test of time.

Based on seven books, hundreds of articles, and 2800 keynote speeches worldwide, I have proven that it is possible to accurately predict the future, but more importantly, I can teach others to do this as well and turn change into an advantage.

Today, we're at a unique tipping point in human history, where we can do things that were impossible just a few years ago. Because of this, it's not enough to be agile solving problems quickly after they happen and innovating in a reactionary way. We need to get out in front and drive positive innovation and change with the confidence certainty can provide, as well as *pre-solve* predictable problems way before they happen.

Pre-solve predictable problems. I like that…

Yes. If you are waiting for problems to happen and then solve them as a reaction to the problem, the number of problems in the future will pile up on you and bury you. The key is to pre-solve them before they happen.

First, you need to be able to separate hard trends from soft trends. Once you do this, you can see future problems and solve them before they happen.

Going back to soft trends, imagine that you're managing a city and working with smart signage, new ways of parking, and so on. The question is, Will you add networked intelligence to make these things smart? The tools are there to do it, but I can't accurately predict that you or someone else will decide to do it or not. The tools to do it are there and represent hard trends; they will happen. Whether you decide to transform your business processes, that is up to you; that is a soft trend.

Too many companies think that most of the future is unpredictable. However, this is a dangerous misconception and is a problem in our way of thinking. We are most often looking ahead using a rearview mirror mindset much more than the windshield. Most don't have a future mindset based on the new realities. We're too busy solving day-to-day problems. This is one of the biggest problems with most organizations today; they are simply too busy putting out fires to take the actions that will make them more relevant in the years ahead. Today, you can busy yourself right out of business.

I guess that most companies are busy doing business, because that is how they survive. Do you suggest that they stop focusing on their core business and look at the future instead?

No, but you do need to start devoting time to being an opportunity manager, not just a crisis manager reacting to change. You can start by devoting 1 hour per week and asking yourself: What am I certain about? What are the hard trends that are shaping the future?

To understand the hard trends shaping the future, start by creating a list of them and identifying the opportunities for each of them. Ask yourself: Which one could I do that would have the biggest payoff for my company? How can I benefit from this hard trend? Use the Three Digital Accelerators to see when will it happen.

When you start thinking like this, you train your anticipatory mindset. And if you encounter any problems, then you can use another principle I teach, you can take your problems and skip them. I call it *problem-skipping*.

Problem-skipping?

Yes. A problem could be that you don't have a enough staff. Then skip the problem! Use outsourced people, virtualization, and A.I. as much as possible.

Another problem: I don't have the money to do it. Skip the problem! Get the money upfront from an ideal customer to fund what you want to sell them.

The vast majority of problems and barriers are perceived problems. It creates a mental barrier. A big problem for many is their assumption that they can't do something. They think of this assumption as a future fact, but it's not! In other words, we spend too much energy looking at why we can't do it. Try putting the same energy into the belief that you can actually do it.

I would like to go back to the hard trends to make sure that both the readers and I fully understand these.

Look at 4G wireless and what is now being implemented in some areas, 5G wireless. What is a hard trend related to this? We're going to have 6G wireless followed by 7G. It *will* happen and, using my Three Digital Accelerators, we even know when it will happen and how powerful each will be. The accelerators are all advancing tech like this along a predictable exponential curve. Ask yourself, How can our company benefit from knowing this?

Another hard-trend example: Baby Boomers are going to get older, they will not get younger. This *will* happen. We can predict both opportunities and problems based on that. Try it!

In the United States, obesity is predicted to grow as a problem. The same with Alzheimer's. Are these hard trends that can't be changed? No! They are soft trends that we can influence or not; we have a choice.

You can't make advances in artificial intelligence stop or disappear, and you can't make mobility go away. They are hard trends that will just become increasingly powerful, so how can you benefit from this?

Your job as a leader, an innovator, and an entrepreneur is to turn these hard trends into opportunities.

Make the trends come to life. Look at these opportunities for your business and for your customers.

When you start doing this and seeing the future more clearly, pick something that is in alignment with the direction that you're going.

I'm fascinated by the idea and methods around hard trends, because most people think that you can't predict the future and be right.

I have a 35-year record of showing that you can use hard trends to predict much of the future and be correct, and you can learn to do this as well. Here is a simple example of a future fact: the stock market will not go up forever; at some point it will go down and then back up. Do you think that I'm right? Yes, because of the science of cycles.

There are more than 500 known cycles. But there is another kind of predictable change; it's linear in that it is not a cycle, it is going in one direction, and it's exponential in its speed. Once you get a smartphone, you're not going back to a "dumb" phone. Smartphones will get smarter. They will have more capabilities, not less. I know this for a fact. You know this for a fact.

Your way of thinking reminds me of the beautiful serenity prayer:

God grant me the serenity
To accept the things I cannot change;
Courage to change the things I can;
And wisdom to know the difference.

Very true. My passion is to wake people up to the fact that you can learn to see more than enough of what is up ahead to make a significant difference in your organization and your life. And we can use that knowledge to shape a better future for all.

Over the decades, working with executives around the world, I've collected thousands of hard trends for my clients. And we've used them to transform their businesses. I started out as a researcher and I taught biology and physics. In other words, I've applied scientific principles to forecasting. Most futurists make educated guesses about the future and call them trends. My hard-trend methodology is changing how companies plan and innovate. You can do this as well.

Let us try looking at a very hyped thing at the moment and applying your methodology to it: self-driving cars. Elon Musk and others talk about them all the time. How will I know as a company when this will happen and what it will mean for my business?

I help companies become *anticipatory organizations*. This means following a number of principles—one of these being the *both/and principle*—when it comes to looking at technology.

Typically, we tend to think in either/or terms about new technology. Either the cars of the future will all be fully autonomous or this will not happen.

Using this principle, you will see that we will have both semiautonomous and autonomous vehicles in the future; it will depend on the use. For example, can you imagine Porsche selling a car without a steering wheel? Their customers like to drive, but as a Porsche customer, I don't like accidents. So, in this case, Porsche will use this tech to eliminate the accident part of driving and at the same time let you drive when you want to drive. It's both/and.

Better to ask, What is the *ideal* place for real autonomous vehicles? I predict very large companies with giant campuses and multiple buildings. Vehicles going from building to building. Buses are another great example, because they follow the same route and stop at the same places. It's not all or nothing. It's both/and.

Finally, I want to understand your principle of *flash foresight*, which was the name of your last book. What is that?

Flash foresight is the concept of using my principles to see the invisible and do the impossible. Humans have been doing impossible things ever since they set foot on the planet. We have created glasses, chairs, jet engines. Things that were at one time thought to be impossible.

How do you do impossible things? The answer is that when a solution to a seemingly impossible problem becomes visible, or when an invisible opportunity becomes visible, you get a flash of foresight that lets you move forward from where you were previously stuck.

What I want people to do is not be passive and hope for a better future. Hope is not a strategy. I want people to actively shape the future! And I want people to think big about their future and then realize that they just thought small. Never to the big, always to the bigger big. Let's actively shape a better future together, and let's do it today! You can learn more by going to www.Burrus.com.

SANDJA BRÜGMANN
The future leader is ethical, passionate, bold, and driven by purpose

Sandja Brügmann (Denmark) is a sustainable leadership, communication, and conscious business expert and international speaker. She was named one of the world's leadership gurus by the Danish Executive Leadership Association. She is founder and managing partner of the Passion Institute and has worked with companies such as Sustainable Brands, Crocs, The Body Shop, and Global Fund for Women.

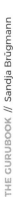

In the future, only the brands that work to make life better for humanity will survive. Therefore, the leaders we appoint to guide us must also be found among those who can create better lives. Hence, tomorrow's leaders must be recruited among society's most ethical, empathetic, innovative, bold, and conscious leaders.

It's not just important to our well-being in the short term but necessary for our survival as human beings that economic and business models that enhance life become the norm. A recent survey shows that 68% of people believe that the most successful brands will be those that make the most positive contribution to society (IPSOS, "Global Trends Survey 2017").

Sustainability: Good for business profit, planet, and people

However, sustainability is not simply a question of ethics. It's good business. The Business and Sustainable Development Commission 2017 estimates that sustainability would be a $12 trillion-a-year market opportunity by meeting the UN's 17 Sustainable Development Goals in just 4 out of 60 sectors—food and agriculture, cities, energy and materials, and health and well-being. To transform the foundation of what is perceived as successful business requires courageous, ethical, and bold leaders who are global systems thinkers and who are willing to experiment, engaging all our human knowledge capacities—not just the rational ability, as is the case in business today.

We need to encourage and elect leaders who create participation-based shared value, organizationally distributed power, and demand and stand for individual autonomy, where the glue of motivation and performance is choice through shared-purpose collaborations and the passionate engagement of individuals.

With ethical responsibility as the pivot for leaders and employees in the business community and the educational system, among our political leaders, and right at the nucleus of our family structures, where each of us take responsibility for own conscious development, we have the possibility of correcting our present skewed course. The future will be about making choices that make life better for ourselves and everyone with whom we are in contact.

A wise leader first and foremost knows himself well, has worked inwards, has been through guilt, shame, and old emotional inhibitions, and presents him- or herself as a complete person who has values and is passionate and driven by a sense of purpose. The fortifying so-called feminine qualities are brought into play with the present, more "masculine" leadership characteristics—so empathy, presence, focus on *us* instead of *me*, together with profit and how we make a difference for people and the environment, all play together. Authentic leaders are visionary, think long term, are bold, and dare to disapprove of ideas—even though they may seem attractive in the short term. They are ethnocentric, have high emotional intelligence (EQ), walk in front, and are examples of how it *can* be done. This requires great willpower, steadfastness, a good ability to set limits, and competent, clear communication. Co-creation, co-action, and collaboration are in focus, and choices are based on what is good for me, good for you, and good for everyone else affected. That will be the key to future-proofing us environmentally, health-wise, economically, and socially.

A couple of known examples of this new type of leader are Canada's prime minister, Justin Trudeau, the business moguls Richard Branson, founder of Virgin, and John Mackey, co-founder of Whole Foods Market, who advocates for *conscious capitalism*, which among other things has established its own Academy of Conscious Leadership to promote the development of authentic and conscious leadership in the company. Lorna Davis, CEO of DanoneWave, the largest US public benefit company, aspires to achieve B Corp certification by 2020. "In 10 years time, people will say it's inconceivable that business was done any other way," says Davis. "The notion that a company can only care about profit will be seen as old fashioned and irresponsible."

It's not only the known leaders and top business managers who must shoulder the responsibility for future-proofing mankind. They simply can't do it alone. It's everybody's responsibility that we become better and more conscious leaders of ourselves, our lives, our work, and our families—every day.

Passionate involvement

There are many potential paths to success, but all require one essential ingredient: *passion.*

In a system that controls or manipulates the individual, passion is squashed, whereas passion gushes forth when people experience an environment of psychological safety, where they can be themselves, fully. At first impression, this seems straightforward, but it's easier said than done, because it requires a society that focuses on cultivating and celebrating the individual person's authenticity.

Sustainable leaders understand that the more backing, freedom, and support people get to be authentic, the better they feel about themselves, which means they are more passionate, contribute with more creative solutions and innovations, and provide great value to their companies and society. The opposite is the case when recognition is lacking and when people are ruled by control and fear; people become absent-minded and indifferent, lacking in vitality and ill in body and spirit. Society doesn't benefit from the innovative and creative involvement of these individuals. It is expensive for society when people are not alive and able to realize themselves—in the short term because they are not contributing, and in the long term because it can lead to long-term costly illnesses, and so on.

The statistics speak their own clear language. People are more absent, uncommitted, stressed, and ill than ever before. Gallup studies in the United States show that approximately half of the American labor workforce is disengaged, which costs the American economy $380 billion a year. Authentic leaders recognize people and boost each person's authentic commitment and value. This is good for the economy, society, and the individual.

Purpose: Vital to the individual, society, and the environment

Companies or organizations that work with meaningfulness at the core of their DNA have a greater purpose, with their existence far beyond selling a product or a service. And because of this, they attract more motivated and engaged labor, as employees intentionally choose a place of work that matches their own values and passion. Deeper meaning is what employees and leaders alike crave. Studies show that 77% of the new millennial generation choose to work for meaningful companies (Deloitte Millennial survey).

A popular place for both work and shopping is the American social enterprise eyewear company Warby Parker, lead by co-founder Neil Blumenthal. Cool eyeglasses at reasonable prices are designed here, and for every purchase, the company donates a pair of glasses to one of the almost one billion people around the world who need glasses. Fifteen percent of the world's population can't see and therefore can't learn or work.

Shades of green

In my work, I frequently meet leaders who are afraid to communicate their company values openly, even though they are authentic, honest, ethical, environmentally progressive, socially conscious, and managerially authentic, because we live in a shame-based culture that condemns everything that isn't perfect. It's so easy to point fingers and criticize others for any perceived mistake. Instead, everyone ought to look more closely at his or her own behavior.

If we are to be successful in creating a society where authenticity is a priority—which is something that we need drastically—then it is essential that we drop the need for perfectionism and praise the imperfect and honest process toward progress. If we are to be successful with this vision, we need a culture and human understanding that makes room for innovation, experimentation, mistakes, and learning. We need a learning process that allows for success, as it is actually quite rare that success is created without trial and error. Being part of—and allowing—a situation based on our own and others' vulnerability and human imperfection requires strength. Let our objective be progress, not perfectionism.

"Have no fear of perfection... You'll never reach it."
—Salvador Dali

The good leader changes the perception of the successful life to support regenerative behaviors that support human thriving, the planet's ability to regenerate itself, and financial profits.

In the near future, humanity will reject the way things have been done hitherto and will demand bold, regenerative, empathetic leadership of itself and everybody in all facets of business, education, politics—all the way into the core of our own families. A society and an existence where success isn't just measured in profit, but in five Ps: passion, purpose, people, planet, and profit.

AUTHENTIC
LEADERSHIP

INTRODUCTION

Welcome to the third and last pillar of *The GuruBook*: *authentic leadership*.

The term *authenticity* has been the subject of study and interpretation right back to the time of the Greek philosophers and the works of, for example, William Shakespeare ("To thine own self be true."—Polonius in *Hamlet*) and other great artists and thinkers.

For Shakespeare, authenticity was the ability to be in control of one's own life and to be in a position to "know yourself."

Construction of the bridge from the "forefathers of authenticity" to today's management philosophies began back in the 1960s, when authenticity was described as the way in which an organization could reflect itself (and its self-identity) through leadership. Back in the 1960s, some people believed that an entire organization—in line with an individual—could act authentically through responsibility, the response to uncertainty, and through creativity. Others believed that authentic leadership was more about the leader's ability to define his or her role in an organization.

Since then, several of the contributors to *The GuruBook* have tried to pin down what authentic leadership is and, not least, how it manifests itself in practice. It can still be difficult to agree on a single definition of authentic leadership, but there does seem to be a number of characteristics that are common to the gurus' contributions and in other knowledge about it. These characteristics are made up of a clear awareness of one's own strengths, limitations, and feelings, to name a few factors. In addition, the authentic leader is driven by a purpose, but this purpose is just as much the organization's as it is the individual leader's.

However, I do not see my role as editor as one that should interpret and expound the gurus' contributions as one or more definitive truths. I will therefore once more (and far preferably) let them have their say. Enjoy yourself with the book's final theme, *authentic leadership*.

TODD DEWETT
The case for authenticity

Dr. Dewett (United States) is one of the world's most watched leadership personalities. He is an authenticity expert, bestselling author at LinkedIn Learning and Lynda.com, a TEDx speaker, and an *Inc.* magazine Top 100 leadership speaker.

For many years, there has been a lot of talk about the essence of leadership. Thinkers of all varieties have offered up their list of basic elements, forgotten secrets, and magic ingredients. Their essays and models speak of things such as trust, service, self-reflection, integrity, and so on. Without a doubt, these are very important concepts.

However, after years of research, reflection, and coaching I have concluded they are all wrong. There is only one foundational catalyst that helps the other concepts spring to life in practice: *authenticity*. In an interpersonal context, authenticity refers to a mixture of consistent honesty, candor, and personal sharing. You can think of it as "being real" or "showing your humanity."

Like many constructs, authenticity exists on a spectrum. Too many of us exist at the low end. We don't speak up. We choose not to share our real views. We feel anxiety about being open and truthful. A smaller group strives for the other end of the spectrum. They share pointed perspectives and personal stories. They talk about life almost as much as they talk about business. They often discuss and laugh at the mistakes we all endure.

Thankfully, this form of frankness and openness most often elicits strong authenticity in response. Thus the fire is started; rapport has begun. Trust may now grow, a service mentality becomes genuine, self-reflection becomes effective, integrity is noticed, and so on.

For such a powerful elixir, surely the cost must be high. No. Authenticity does not cost you as much as an executive training program, not as much as a weekend seminar, and not even as much as a good leadership book. It's free—if you have patience and the guts to open up a little.

So let's consider the case for authenticity.

Too much of a good thing can hurt

Social decorum matters. Putting your best foot forward is important. Understanding contextual norms is vital. In short, smart people know they must manage impressions, especially at work. That's a good thing, right?

Managing impressions involves some combination of the following: talking about one's accomplishments and awards, refraining from saying anything that might be risky or references one's imperfections, complimenting others, feigning interest where there is none, and censoring disagreement or disgust in order to show respect or to preserve group harmony.

All of these are understandable in small amounts on occasion. However, they are typically very common, if not heavily overindulged. The result is serious. You successfully share a limited, overly biased, and somewhat plastic version of yourself. You maintain largely uninformed views of others at work. The ultimate outcome is stale, minimally satisfying, and minimally productive relationships.

We are starving for authentic connection

We are naturally wired to desire real connections with other humans. This is partially why we love family and friends so dearly. This human need is seen as fundamental, right along with the need for food and safety. We need to belong. We need to have our voice heard. We need to feel that our most common human interactions matter and that they are not fake or overly contrived.

Unfortunately, too many people believe that at work you are to be "professional" and at home you can be "personal"; never shall the two meet. Common sense and the social sciences now agree: this is not a useful perspective. To be clear, you are not trying to make friends with everyone at work. That is unrealistic and potentially dangerous. You are, however, supposed to strive to be more than merely professional. A little intentional authenticity amplifies your professional potential immensely. People want to believe in the person, not just the professional.

We fear that which makes us great

It takes a truly massive effort to reverse a natural human tendency. We are born with a strong desire to try new things, to explore, and to seek deep connections with others. Don't believe me? Spend 5 minutes with a small child and you are sure to remember. When the child falls, they simply get up. When they break something, they keep moving. The exploration continues with glee. It's the adults who make this process difficult and unnatural.

These same adults often say predictable things when talking about the virtues of humanity. They mention only bravery, strength, accomplishments, and other positive and safe notions. This, of course, is a very incomplete view of who we are. They passionately disavow the other half of the human experience: the mistakes, failures, uncertainties, and doubts.

Yet it's these more difficult concepts that ultimately make us great. Surely, great thoughts and great learning are fueled by our mistakes and failures. We must remember what that child within us knows about what it means to be human. You can unleash that child by helping realize the fears are false.

There is no monster under the bed

You have been told by an army of people that certain things are bad and to be avoided: failure, mistakes, setbacks, and so on. The army is vast: parents, neighbors, teachers, colleagues, and bosses. Over time, they beat you into submission and convince you there is a monster under your bed. It looms ever present, claws out, ready to pounce on you and make you consume another dose of self-hatred, fear, doubt, and shame.

In truth, there is no monster under the bed. Stated more honestly, that thing under the bed is actually your friend, possibly your best friend in life. What the successful people in life have taught us is that failure is an inevitable positive part of the learning process. Mistakes happen. Things don't work out. So what? Everyone experiences these things. What differentiates the successful from the rest of us is how passionately they learn and grow as a result. They don't ignore the monster. They don't tame the monster. They make friends.

Step one on the path to success is embracing authenticity. Don't get me wrong; it's not risk free. Some will always cling to the false distinction between "professional" and "personal." You don't need them. The more you take the risk of being authentic—honest, open, vulnerable—the more you attract authentic people and the more your tribe grows.

Start with yourself

Perhaps changing society is not within your reach, or maybe it is. In either case, what is clear is that you can have a strong influence on your immediate context.

Start with a desire to increase your personal authenticity. You must consciously choose to bring more of the complete and raw you into every new situation. Through self-reflection, begin to take an inventory of how you're doing. When are you good at being real? When do you tend to censor and why? The more you become aware and focused, the faster you gain comfort being you and the less you feel compelled to manage impressions.

Next, begin to intentionally model authenticity for others. Start slow and safe by just putting one toe into the water. Ask them about what they really think. Throw out a challenging perspective on a work topic and let them react. Ask them about their children. Tell them about a book that really moved you. As you begin to filter yourself a little less, others will reciprocate and deeper connections become possible.

When others say something brave, don't just offer a reaction, tell them you respect the bravery of their position. If someone mentions their weekend plans, be inquisitive. If they admit a vulnerability or recall a difficult moment, let them know how much you appreciate the gesture. Ask them about it. Seek to understand. Show appreciation. Reciprocate by slowly lowering your wall.

Choose one person

Your authenticity journey is a marathon, not a sprint. Consider starting with just one person in mind. It might be a colleague, your boss, a mentor, or even a client or vendor. Chose to find a new, more honest way to let your humanity show when interacting with them. It might be a question, a topical focus you adopt, a comment about one of your interests, or just your curiosity about some aspect of who they are. Go slow and gain a new level of comfort with that one person. Then try another person.

You might be surprised what you learn when you lower your defenses and reveal a little more of who you are as a person. After comfort, it may even become fun. Before long, you'll be jumping off of the bed regularly to play with that friend hiding beneath. It will change how you view your potential and the potential of those around you—and it doesn't cost a penny!

THIS ABOVE ALL: TO THINE OWN
SELF BE TRUE, AND IT MUST
FOLLOW, AS THE NIGHT THE DAY,
THOU CANST NOT THEN BE
FALSE TO ANY MAN.

Shakespeare

EDGAR H. SCHEIN
Knowing why you are there

Edgar Schein (United States) is the Society of Sloan Fellows Professor of Management Emeritus and a Professor Emeritus at the MIT Sloan School of Management. Schein investigates organizational culture, process consultation, research process, career dynamics, and organization learning and change. He is a recipient of the Distinguished Scholar-Practitioner Award of the Academy of Management and the 2012 recipient of the Lifetime Achievement Award from the International Leadership Association.

It is all well and good to be invited to write something as a "guru." Presumably, that is supposed to mean that with all of your 88 years of experience you should know something to pass on to younger people. At the same time, you realize that the older and presumably wiser you are, the less confident you are about wisdom, truth, and knowledge. What is wisdom anyway? More facts, more skills, more caution, more resilience, more agility, and, perhaps most of all, more humility. Maybe the hardest thing to discover in life is how fragile you are, how much of what happens is out of your control, and in fact, how dependent you really are on others.

As I think about humility, I am also reminded of a persistent question I could not answer: How come some people clearly have more "presence" than others? How come some people are noticed immediately when they enter a room, while others are not noticed at all? This question bothered me because I often felt I was not noticed until someone introduced me, gave me a platform, silenced the room on my behalf. How come some

people can do this for themselves, can create their own platform, be present from the moment they enter a new situation, whether that be a classroom, a party, or even a crowd of strangers. Personality characteristics such as extraversion–introversion, social ascendance, assertiveness, and emotional intelligence did not cut it for me. Those might all play a role, but deep down I felt there was something else in presence that we had not yet figured out.

Then, one year, I was having a conversation with a fellow organization development consultant and brought up this topic because I had learned that this man, lets call him John, was also a successful part-time actor. I turned the topic to the question of whether this "presence" issue was important in the craft of acting, to which he replied with some intensity that it was "all important." An actor must have presence in front of an audience or camera or things will not go well. So, naturally, I followed up with the question, "What does it take for an actor to be present?"

A long pause followed. John wondered out loud about the same question and gradually worked out his answer. He said that he was currently in a play where he had a tiny part. He was the butler who had to make an announcement of someone's arrival. And it was thinking about this bit part that revealed to him the answer: as he was getting ready to step on the stage and deliver his line, *he had to know why he was there.*

He had to know his lines, of course, but more importantly, he had to know and understand the play, the scene, the importance of the announcement, and the consequences if he fouled up in some way. He said that if he did not get into that mental state of fully knowing why he was there, he could not confidently step out on that stage and deliver his line correctly.

I thought deeply about the implications of this simple principle. I remembered immediately that when I went to a cocktail party "just to see who was there and mingle," I was much more anxious than when I went to that same party in order to meet my wife who was already there and who was going to introduce me to one of her friends. I wondered whether my entry in the first situation was less noticeable than my entry in the second situation. Did I have more presence when I knew what I was doing, had a purpose and a specific goal—in other words, knew why I was there?

Life is a series of situations, some of which we can predict and some of which just overwhelm us. I was given an honorary degree at the Bled School of Management in Slovenia and knew that I was supposed to give some kind of talk after receiving the degree. I had prepared a talk with PowerPoint and thought I was prepared, but when I arrived a day before the ceremony, I discovered we were in a big hall, there would be many nonacademics there, and giving my talk would be absolutely the wrong thing

to do. I was quite anxious but also knew that just rewriting a short talk was out of the question. I asked myself, "Why am I here? What is this situation? What is expected of me?" I gradually realized the ritualized ceremonial nature of the event and that what would be expected of me was a few simple words of thanks and, perhaps, a simple message that would "justify" the honor of being given the degree. There were no scripted lines, but I knew that "some wise words" were expected from the honoree.

I ran through a lot of stuff that had been in my talk and finally found something worth mentioning—how leaders communicate their values through their actions. This was, however, a pretty pedestrian message and I knew I was there to say something more, something provocative, something new. But what? It came to me as I was preparing to be called to the stage to receive my robe, my hood, and my degree, and it ended up being quite a satisfactory, powerful message. I felt I had presence and had something to say and was very grateful at having been able to "rise to the occasion."

The message itself was important and relevant—that leaders communicate their values more by what they do *not* say and do than by what they *do* say and do. Perhaps the most powerful example I had observed over and over again was how leaders did not notice that their failure to ask personal questions of their subordinates showed their lack of interest in those subordinates and led to some of the disengagement that those same leaders later complained about. I challenged the audience to think about this and said silently to myself, "What a relief that I had discovered what I was there for and had not bored them with my long lecture."

Since that conversation with John, the actor, I have explored how widely applicable his simple principle is. I have noticed, for example, that doctors in a teaching hospital who lecture to the residents about the case in front of the patient get much less good information than those who believe they are there to form a relationship with the patient and who concentrate on their conversation with the patient rather than with the residents. I have noticed that managers who think they are there to help their subordinates perform better than managers who think they are there to tell subordinates what to do.

The form in which you present yourself comes across to others. If you are not interested in them, they will sense this, as every therapist and consultant will confirm. Presence is about purpose and goals, not about personal style or personality. If you know why you are there, if you have figured out your role in the total situation, if you know your lines, you will have presence. It turns out to be as simple as that.

DARE TO DECLARE WHO YOU
ARE. IT IS NOT FAR FROM THE
SHORES OF SILENCE TO THE
BOUNDARIES OF SPEECH.
THE PATH IS NOT LONG, BUT
THE WAY IS DEEP. YOU MUST
NOT ONLY WALK THERE, YOU
MUST BE PREPARED TO LEAP.

Hildegard Von Bingen

BART HOULAHAN
I want to redefine success in business

Bart Houlahan (United States) is co-founder of the B Corp movement and a social, serial entrepreneur. Prior to B Lab, Houlahan was president of AND 1, a $250 million footwear company. He is a Henry Crown Fellow of the Aspen Institute and a recipient of both the 2014 Skoll Award for Social Entrepreneurship and the 2015 John P. McNulty Prize.

You might have heard about the B Corp movement. If not, that's going to change soon. Currently, entrepreneur Bart Houlahan and his team are expanding across the globe with their message that we need to redefine success in business.

Bart, along with his partners Jay Coen Gilbert and Andrew Kassoy, co-founded B Lab. The organization behind the B Corp movement has certified more than 2000 leading sustainable businesses as certified B Corporations, and the B Lab impact management tools have been used by more than 60,000 companies across the globe.

I sat down and talked to Bart about his work with the movement and how we might be at a tipping point in the evolution of capitalism.

I've read that you see a big change in business culture and business purpose going on right now—on a number of different levels. Can you please explain more about these different levels?

I think we're moving out of an economic model with an exclusive focus on shareholders to one that is more focused on stakeholders.

This is due to a number of global changes going on right now. For example, consumers have different expectations of companies than they used to have. A recent study showed that 88% of all consumers expect business leaders to balance the needs of their company with the needs of society in general. This is very different than just a few decades ago.

I also see a growing interest in investing capital in companies that focus on stakeholders and not just shareholders. Since 2008, the growth within sustainable investments has been substantial. It's one of the fastest-growing trends right now in a number of countries and markets.

Finally, I think that we're experiencing a cultural shift too. The next generation of employees expect more of their leaders and their jobs than they used to. They want more than money; they want a meaningful job, a job with purpose. It's a very different expectation from what companies are delivering to their employees currently.

You describe this change as going on within consumers, investors, and workers. What about policymakers?

I think that we're seeing governments on a global level expecting more from businesses as well. Both the left and the right agree that the private sector needs to get more involved in solving some of the world's biggest problems.

Now, you explain some very positive trends, but how does the B Corp mindset and method fit into all this?

A B Corporation is a company that is both making money and making a difference. We're focused on a for-profit model that creates shared value alongside shareholder value.

Our role is also very focused on delivering standards to differentiate a good company from just good marketing. There are more and more companies claiming to be purpose-driven, green, and socially responsible, but unless you have standards to back this up, it all becomes too blurry and meaningless.

One of the core focuses of our role as an organization is therefore to make these things tangible. Individually, B Corps meet the highest standards of verified social and environmental performance, public transparency, and legal accountability, and aspire to use the power of markets to solve social and environmental problems.

Collectively, B Corps lead a growing global movement of people using business as a force for good. Through the power of their collective voice, we hope that all companies will one day compete to be the best for the world, and society will enjoy a more shared and durable prosperity for all.

So B Corps is not really about you guys, B Lab?

No. We view ourselves as a service agency for leaders who are truly creating impact, our entrepreneurs. There's a reason why you may not have seen a lot of articles about us or about the nonprofit B Lab. It's quite intentional; we exist to serve entrepreneurs who are using businesses as a force for good. If we do not serve those entrepreneurs, we don't create any impact. The real work is being done by the community of certified B Corporations who are creating completely innovative solutions for some of the world's greatest challenges.

Are all B Corps then based on products that make the world a better place?

No. You should not confuse purpose with product. We cover more than 150 industries, and for us, purpose is a broader definition than just your service or product. It's more about the impact that is being created—who you employ, how you source your products, your ownership structure, and so on.

We're a very diverse community. We have B Corps that are multi-billion-dollar companies and we have small startups. We generally believe all types of business can be a force of good, as long as the intention of the business is broader than just creating private wealth for individuals.

Purpose is a very broad term that can mean basically anything within the business world. But you're not really looking for more purpose-driven companies in the future then?

We love companies with a deep and meaningful purpose, but our focus is different. I believe that the shareholder primacy theory has to change. If the rule of the market is exclusively focused on a single beneficiary—the shareholder—it is difficult to see how a market solution can solve all the great challenges that we're facing at the moment.

However, I'm not against capitalism. I'm skeptical toward the current perversion of the capitalist system. In my view, capitalism was not inherently built to exclusively build private wealth. Companies were originally intended to contribute to society more broadly and lift all boats.

If I understand you correctly, you're advocating for businesses that are using the operations of their organization to lift all stakeholders. Correct?

Yes, and this can be done is a vast number of ways. As an example, many incredible B Corporations might not necessarily be contributing to the environment with their core product, but they still create positive change through their work with stakeholders.

I'm not looking to build a movement only consisting of social entrepreneurs. I'm in this to redefine success in business.

When you talk about redefining success in business, you're also saying that we currently don't measure what really matters. But isn't this a subjective thing?

No. I believe that you can always build a better business—better for your workers, the community, and the environment. And "better" is not merely a subjective thing.

Our way of making this more objective is, among other things, to create an online assessment tool that will walk you through a series of questions to help you learn what it takes to make things better. We ask you questions related to government, workers, community, and the environment. Examples of these could be as follows:

- What portion of your management is evaluated in writing on their performance with regard to corporate, social, and environmental targets?
- Based on referenced compensation studies, how does your company's compensation structure (excluding executive management) compare with the market?
- Which is the broadest community with whom your environmental reviews/audits are formally shared?

Early on, as we talked with hundreds of entrepreneurs, there was clarity that they wanted to be a positive alternative, that being defined by what they were not wasn't a great way to build a movement. So on the impact assessment, you don't earn any negative points. Instead, we're offering a positive alternative for investors, consumers, and policymakers to support. I think it has served this movement well to position our core identity as being the positive alternative.

What is your final goal with this organization? To create a world full of certified B Corps?

No, we're trying to create a *leadership play* that will influence mainstream business. We're focusing on the top 10% in every geography and industry. We want to identify, support, and celebrate these B Corp leaders and hope they will inspire legions of other companies to follow. We want to leave a mark.

HENRY MINTZBERG
Companies with soul[1]

Dr. Henry Mintzberg (Canada) is an internationally renowned academic, author, and researcher. He has written 180 articles and 19 books, and in 1994, he published his groundbreaking *The Rise and Fall of Strategic Planning*. Today, Mintzberg helps many organizations with their strategic processes, and in 2015, he published *Rebalancing Society*, where his efforts are now concentrated.

My daughter Lisa once left me a note in a shoe that read, "Souls need fixing." Little did she know…

A tale of two nurses

When we asked the members of our new health-care management class (imhl.org) to share stories about their experiences, an obstetrician told one about the time when, as a resident, he was shuttling between the wards of different hospitals. One stood out: he and his colleagues "loved working there." It was a "happy" place, thanks to a head nurse who cared. She was understanding, respectful of everyone, intent on promoting collaboration between doctors and nurses. The place had soul.

Then she retired and was replaced by someone very qualified in nursing, with an MBA. Without "any conversation … she started questioning everything." She was strict with the nurses—for example, arriving early to check who came late. Where there used to be chatting and laughing before the start of shifts, "it became normal for us to see one nurse crying" because of some comment by the boss.

Morale plummeted, and soon that spread to the physicians: "It took 2–3 months to destroy that amazing family…. We used to compete to go to that hospital; [then] we didn't want to go there any more." Yet "the higher authority didn't intervene or maybe was not aware" of what was going on. They were no better.

The epidemic

How often have you heard such a story, or worse, experienced one? In the work that I do—studying management and organizations—I hear them often (in a recent week, four times). And no few are about CEOs. Managing without soul has become an epidemic in society—managers who specialize in killing cultures at the expense of human engagement.

---

[1] This appeared originally as "The epidemic of managing without soul," 21 May 2015, on the author's TWOG: TWeet2blOG, @mintzberg141 or mintzberg.org/blog.

There are schools that teach this, but I won't name names for fear of insulting colleagues in prominent places. Out of them come graduates with a distorted impression of management: detached, generic, technocratic. They are taught to believe they can manage anything, whether or not they have serious knowledge of the context. This technocratic detachment is bad enough—numbers, numbers, numbers. The worst of it is also mean-spirited—bullying people and playing them off against each other. One person, bullied for years by a nasty boss, said, "It's the little things that wear you down." These managers care for nothing but themselves.

Why do we tolerate this? Why do we allow narcissists with credentials, posing as leaders, to bring down so many of our institutions? Souls need fixing all right.

Part of the problem is that people are generally selected into managerial positions by "superiors" (senior managers, boards of directors), often with no idea about the damage caused by their decisions. And so we often get what have been called "kiss up and kick down" managers—terribly able to impress "superiors," while terribly incapable of respecting "subordinates."

A hotel with soul

Last week, I was in England for meetings about our International Masters in Practicing Management program (impm.org; it's been designed to reverse this epidemic). We stayed at one of those corporate hotels; I hated it from years ago—no spirit, no soul. I recall the high turnover of staff, and one year, they charged our Japanese participants $10 per minute for calls back home—minutes that a participant from British Telecom estimated to cost the hotel pennies.

Lisa is in England, and so after the meetings we went travelling in the Lake District, a great place to hike. The IMPM is to run in October in a hotel there that we haven't used before, so Lisa and I volunteered to check it out.

I walked in and fell in love with the place. Beautifully appointed, perfectly cared for, and genuinely attentive staff—this place was loaded with soul. I've been in the business of studying organizations for so long that I can often walk into a place and sense soul, or no soul, in an instant. I can feel the energy of the place, or the lethargy—the instant smile instead of some grin from a "greeter," honest concern instead of programmed "care." ("We appreciate your business!" as you wait for someone to answer the phone. This means "Our time is more important than yours.")

"What's it mean to have soul?" Lisa asked.
"You know it when you see it," I replied. In every little corner.
I asked a waiter about hiking trails. He didn't know, so he fetched the manager of the hotel to tell me. I chatted with a young woman at reception. "The throw pillows on the bed are really beautiful," I said.
"Yes," she replied, "the owner cares for every detail—she picked those pillows herself."
"How long have you been here?" I asked.
"Four years," she said proudly, and then rattled off the tenures of the senior staff: the manager 14 years, the assistant manager 12 years, the head of sales a little less, and so on.

Why can't all organizations be like this? Most people—employees, customers, managers—want to care, given half a chance. We human beings have souls, and so too can our hospitals and hotels. Why do we build so many great institutions only to let them wither under the control of people who should never have been allowed to manage anything? Management needs fixing all right, and so do the souls of our societies.

THOMAS D. ZWEIFEL
No idols > authentic vision

Dr. Thomas D. Zweifel (Switzerland) is a strategy and performance expert, leadership professor, TED speaker, and coach for leaders of Global 1000 companies. Zweifel is the award-winning author of seven books, including the bestsellers *Communicate or Die*, *Strategy-in-Action*, and *The Rabbi and the CEO*, on which this chapter is based. He has served as CEO of Swiss Consulting Group (1997–2013), and since 2001, he has taught leadership at Columbia University and St. Gallen University.

"The idols of the nations are silver and gold, human handiwork."

Psalms 135:15–16

"I don't want to achieve immortality through my work.
I want to achieve immortality through not dying."

Woody Allen

The Second Commandment says, "You shall not make yourself a carved image." Are you worshiping idols? Acting out someone else's dream or expectation? Money, power, fame—or guruhood—are not goals; they are only a means to an end. A leader's true vision is larger than life, includes many others, and often outlives the leader. What legacy will you leave behind? This article is excerpted from Zweifel's award-winning book, *The Rabbi and the CEO*.

Moses returned to camp and was in for a shock: The people had made a golden calf. They had turned the infinite essence into a thing and prayed to gold. Moses acted decisively: He smashed the tablets and had 3000 of the idolaters killed.[1]

Why did Moses intervene with such holy fury? Because idols lead people astray from their authentic mission. The Commandment "You shall have no idols" is about focusing on the future without being distracted by short-term gratification or glory. And yet we live at a time when many seem to have their eye on the wrong ball: themselves and their stuff. Back in 1967, a survey of college students found that their highest priority was "a meaningful philosophy of life."[2] By 2006, more than 80% listed "wealth" as their top priority, with "fame" as a close second. Shows like *American Idol* or *Germany's Next Top Model* epitomize this trend.

Nothing wrong with wealth or fame; but they are side-effects at best, and at worst false gods. Famous billionaires like Gates or Buffett, Bloomberg or Oprah did not get there by wanting stardom or billions; they each committed to their own vision of adding value. For that, a leader's vision must be larger than self-interest.

Judaism is inextricably linked to the vision of a brilliant future; the Promised Land—or the Messiah—is its very essence. So unsurprisingly, the Bible is filled with visionaries like Isaiah who castigated leaders ("O my people, your leaders mislead you, and they have corrupted the direction of your ways"[3]), but just as easily conjured up stirring visions of peace ("They shall beat their swords into plowshares and … no longer study warfare"[4]). Training of prophets was even institutionalized in schools. The investment paid off: While only 48 male and seven female prophets (yes, women broke through the glass ceiling then) are named, there were over *1.2 million* prophets in Jewish history.[5]

The Hebrew word for prophet, *navi*, means "words from lips." Twelfth-century Maimonides wrote that a prophet who keeps a vision to him- or herself is liable to the death penalty.[6] No matter how great your vision—if it's not shared, it will die. Jürgen Schrempp's vision for DaimlerChrysler, though hailed as a "merger in heaven," never materialized. Schrempp failed to align Daimler's vision ("Only the Best") with Chrysler's (whatever the customer wants).

Some have little patience for visionaries. Former German chancellor Helmut Schmidt quipped that if people want vision, they should see an eye doctor. (Understandably: Germans were badly burnt and have been skeptical of grand ideas ever since Hitler's delusions.) There is nothing wrong with realists concerned with making reliable predictions. Reducing uncertainty is key to management, and it's only human to wish to lessen the tension between the now and the future you want.

But the only future-oriented statements of realists are soporific forecasts, for example, "After our flat performance last year, we should have 1 percent growth."

Worse, for the realist the future is pretty much an extension of the past.

The Hebrew word for "past," *avar*, has the same root as the word for "sin" or "wrongdoing," *averah*. Moses knew it was easier to take the people out of Egypt than to take Egypt out of the people. As things got tough, many would idealize the way things used to be.[7] But being addicted to the past is the opposite of leadership. Leaders are not merely about changing what is—present circumstances result from yesterday—but about creating what isn't.

No pipe-dreams, though. Isaiah's dream of total peace, or Martin Luther King's that we'll all be brothers one day, is a worthy aspiration but ultimately beyond reach. A vision, to deserve the name, is unpredictable and yet possible to achieve; a magnet for action, it gets people out of bed each morning; a strategic filter, it weeds out irrelevant actions. It should not be exclusively self-serving ("I want $250,000 a year") but inclusive, owned by key stakeholders and implementers. Gates's vision—solving everybody's computer problems everywhere—is all-encompassing; and Jobs famously asked then-Pepsico's John Sculley, "Do you want to spend the rest of your life selling sugared water or do you want a chance to change the world?"

Proverbs warns that "Where there is no vision, people perish."[8] Yet our concerns tend to be short-term: this quarter's stock price, e-mail backlogs or office politics. Many managers spend virtually all their time running the present, not crafting the future. Many of us are caught in business-as-usual. Even if we put out the occasional fire, we react to circumstances; we live from the past—unless we are struck by a shocking change of destiny, like a sudden illness or (in my case) 9/11.

One man had a rude awakening from business-as-usual: Alfred Nobel, who had amassed his fortune through war ammunition. When his brother died,

Nobel's life changed. One newspaper confused the two and believed Alfred was the dead brother. So he got the rare chance to read his own obituary while still being alive. It was not pretty. The article described Nobel as the man responsible for killing more people than anyone in history.

He realized he would be remembered for this death-laden legacy. Loath to leave such a legacy, he established the Nobel Prize, which would become the ultimate honor in literature, science—and peace. Over a century later, Nobel's lasting legacy is not chiefly his contribution to war and death, but to peace and life.

Leaders, in Gandhi's words, must "Be the change we wish the world to make."[9] The Talmud asks, "Who is wise?" and answers: "He who sees what is to be born."[10] Imprisoned for 27 years, Nelson Mandela stood in the future—until finally, impossibly, he became president.

When my client, a tier-one energy company's president, crafted his life vision, one commitment was, "Make people laugh." I was nonplussed. Was this the same intimidating guy who berated subordinates; whose conference calls were deadly corporate torture? Yes, he said. He wanted to tell war stories and corporate jokes on stage. I asked, "Why are you waiting until retirement? How about living that future *now*?" At the Christmas party, managers came up to my table and whispered, "What did you do with him? He is a new man. He cracks us up. He's actually fun to work for!"

That is authentic vision—and authentic leadership.

Notes

1. Deuteronomy 34:10–12.
2. Gene I. Maeroff, "Study Finds Fewer Freshmen in College Look into Teaching," *The New York Times*, January 29, 1983.
3. Isaiah 3:12.
4. Isaiah 3:4.
5. Talmud, Megillah, 14a. According to the Midrash Rabba, Song of Songs 4:11, for every male prophet there was one female prophetess.
6. Moses Maimonides, *Mishneh Torah*, approx. 1170–1180, Chapter 9, Law 3.
7. William Bridges, "Getting Them through the Wilderness: A Leader's Guide to Transition," *New Management*, 1987: 50–55.
8. Proverbs 29:18.
9. Arun Gandhi quoting Mohandas Gandhi, in Michel W. Potts, "Arun Gandhi Shares the Mahatma's Message," in *India-West* (San Leandro, CA, February 1, 2002), Vol. XXVII, No. 13: A34.
10. Tamid 32A.

TRUTH NEVER DAMAGES
A CAUSE THAT IS JUST.

Mahatma Gandhi

CHRISTIAN ØRSTED
Authentic leadership is narcissism

Christian Ørsted (Denmark) is a management consultant, public speaker, and author. His client list includes Mærsk, Novo Nordisk, LEGO, and the Danish Ministry of Foreign Affairs. Ørsted is the author of the bestselling book *Lethal Leadership*.

As soon as I, as the editor of *The GuruBook*, introduced my good friend Christian Ørsted to the theme *authentic leadership*, I could see that he both smiled (as he always does) and had a somewhat skeptical look on his face.

For a long time, Christian has inspired me with his very human and concrete approach to leadership. No matter whether we talk about his bestseller *Lethal Leadership* or his way of public speaking, I have always regarded him as very authentic. I also like the way that he doesn't wrap things up when he, for instance, as in this interview, states that "we can't solve our leadership problems by sending the asshole on a training course."

That was why I thought that Christian could make this book's readers even wiser about the term *authentic leadership*, but as it turned out, the interview moved in another direction. We sat together on a rainy spring day in the Navitas innovation environment in Aarhus, and almost immediately, Christian began puncturing the whole thinking behind authenticity in leadership.

The following interview thus became an exciting and very critical look at authentic leadership.

What is authentic leadership to you, Christian?

Actually, I wish your angle was broader than authenticity. The other two main themes in your book don't have an angle or an adjective. You don't call it "dynamic innovation," but simply "innovation."

But when we talk about leadership, it's as if there's something else, something more involved. This doesn't only apply to *The GuruBook*, but as a whole when we talk about leadership. It's as if some seasoning should be added and that leadership as a subject should be entertaining, inspiring, and likeable instead of substantial, effective, and documented. Imagine speaking of surgery in the same way! If, instead of sharing experiences about what works, we focused on what surgeons think is funny or inspiring to read books about or be trained in.

So *authenticity* is a superfluous word when we talk about leadership, or what? Should we just stop the interview here?

In my view, we talk about authenticity because it's lacking. We're talking out of a longing. When a company hangs posters on its wall with its values and about how authentic or service minded it is, you know precisely what the organization lacks: authenticity and a service mindset. The problem with self-exclaimed authenticity is that it's false. Just as people in the old days believed that people performed better if you gave them unrealistic targets, we must today realize that people don't become more authentic by talking about authenticity. It's a gigantic mistake to focus on results; whether there's a target, or a certain type of authentic behavior, is unimportant. Instead, we should focus on efforts. We must move from talking about *what* we want to achieve to talking about *how* we can support each other in achieving it.

Does this mean that, after all, you do believe that it is relevant to talk about authenticity in the sense that it is a part of good leadership, or what?

In my view, one can happily talk about authenticity, but I don't believe it should be an objective in itself when we talk about leadership. For me, it's far more relevant to talk about propriety—for instance, caring for others and psychological security. Leadership should focus on providing a culture in which you know you can trust each other.

In this way, the leader's most important task is not being authentic but focusing on *serving*. The leader's own idea of the world or of him- or herself is completely without interest with regard to how he or she can serve the organization and the world in the best possible way.

That's why there's a risk that the whole concept of authentic leadership can easily give leaders an excuse for being narcissistic and focusing on themselves and their own values as leaders rather than how they create the best possible culture for their employees.

So the authentic leader is a narcissist?

In my view, there's a need for changing the focus from the individual to the community. Yes, being a leader can be as hard as nails, but that's how it must be if it benefits the community.

It's important to remember that our happiest times as people as a rule are those when we give up something to benefit the community. This happens when we become parents. It happens in relationships and team sports, and it can to a high degree also apply in the managerial suite.

The great focus of our time on the individual leader and the individual man or woman is in my view mistaken and ineffective. There's a lot more to be gained from how good communities function, because these communities will often solve many of the individual problems for people. But we don't solve our leadership problems in an organization by sending an asshole on a training course. Instead, we must focus on what our culture permits, what it encourages, and what consequences there are of short-sighted, egoistic, and self-centered behavior. In many instances we say we must think long term, think about the customers and colleagues, and be humble, but in practice it's the opposite qualities that are rewarded. I think that we all know examples of the loud, self-righteous types who were promoted while the quiet and cautious types, who slaved away in the background, were passed over.

So we should stop sending people on courses and make people like you and me redundant?

In my view, course-based leadership and inspirational leadership don't work. Instead of sending people on these courses, you should focus on the context they are in every day—who they are together with and how they do things there, where they are.

When leaders give an inspiring speech saying now everything will be good, you're hungering for new input just as much as you do after a visit to McDonald's. You return to the same people and the same everyday again.

We should look far more closely at how we carry out our work and who we do it with, and aim at long-term and sustainable changes in the organization.

Part of authentic leadership deals with openness and daring to be oneself and showing one's feelings. Do you not believe that this is important for a leader?

I believe that it is important for a leader to be open about things, but the good leader waits before telling the world outside about these problems until the world outside can deal with them. That means that you as leader make a very conscious decision about what is beneficial to say to the world outside and how you do it.

Let me give you an example from the military, where an officer told me about his managerial breakthrough—in other words, the time when he really got his men's trust. It was after a mission, when he had given orders to kill and had himself killed. When they got back to their camp, he cried in front of his platoon at their after-action debriefing. You can say that's authentic and open—daring to show your feelings—but the most important thing was that he didn't stand crying in a field in the Helmand province, where Taliban warriors could be lying in ambush and kill them all.

No, he waited until they were back in their camp and in that way he put the needs of the group before his own feelings. Therefore, he wasn't just authentic. He was more than that. He could be counted on both in a difficult situation and later in acknowledging how difficult it was. In that way, he gave room so others could also be moved—and exemplified when and how we can support each other best.

It gives food for thought that the military is often mentioned as a pioneer in good leadership. As a pacifist, I won't go deeper into that debate, but it's worth mentioning when we talk about leadership as a discipline. Another contributor to this book, Simon Sinek, also uses the military as an example in his book Leader's Eat Last. His point is that leaders in the American army are rewarded with medals for sacrificing themselves for the community, while in the business community you get bonuses for sacrificing others.

Luckily, it's not like that in all organizations, but I understand well where Sinek is going, and that's precisely why it's so dangerous to advise leaders to be more authentic, open, or vulnerable. It will often turn out to be an impediment for them in their careers, as it is other qualities that are rewarded.

If instead we agreed on and created understanding for rules and the consequences in the community, it would be a big step forward. But there is often a great difference between the agreed rules and the consequences experienced. This isn't just hypocritical, it's also bad business, as it turns the work into a guessing game instead of a place where we can generate value together.

As leaders, we must focus more on what generates value and makes the community function than on our own need to be likeable and popular. That's easy enough when these things go hand in hand, but it's not leadership; leadership is what's called for to make something happen that would not have occurred by itself—that is, when we hold on to something that's bigger than we are.

Earlier in the interview, you mentioned psychological security as something quite central—and more important than authenticity. What does that mean in practice?

Psychological security is the belief that you won't be punished or humiliated for talking about your ideas, questions, concerns, or mistakes. What is essential is the belief. And it's a belief many have lost. They have experienced far too many times that they must be careful about which ideas they air, that asking questions can quickly make them look stupid in others' eyes, and that mistakes are an expression of a lack of competence or diligence—not because the leaders say that, but because that's what they experience in reality when they air new ideas, ask questions, or talk about their mistakes.

In such an organization, you cannot learn, you cannot develop, and everyone is the architect of their own happiness. It's an insecure place to work, and people therefore become—quite rightly—more careful. They become egocentric and oversensitive to the criticism and dialogue that can further them.

Just as we've seen that the right friendships also have room for criticism and errors, because we know we're on the same side, we see that really good

organizations are capable of both celebrating when things go well and developing, and talking about the difficult things, the things that must be changed or aren't good enough.

This can therefore lead to difficult discussions, but what is quite essential is that the people in such organizations know where they have each other. You become far more insecure from not being told things and having to guess whether or not you're doing a good job.

In addition, this form of culture is also meaningful with regard to *The GuruBook*'s second main theme on innovation, as we know that problems can rarely be solved by individuals but are best solved when we are several people working together to fix them.

Therefore, I believe very much in the creative community, where as a leader you create a space in which the employees can talk about problems, what concerns them, which ideas they have, and what they are in doubt about. That is a form of psychological security where you don't feel exposed if you have to raise difficult questions or dare go against the line laid down by the management.

In that respect, I've seen you quoted as saying that resistance to change is a resource in an organization. At first glance, that sounds illogical when we're talking innovation.

The paradox here is that we almost never talk about change management, except when the reality is that we are exposing the employees to cutbacks. In that regard, you often forget that acceptance and resignation resemble each other from the outside. And the worst are those who give up, those who doubt whether it's any use at all.

If we can increase the psychological security in the organization, we enable people to say what makes the change better and more effective. That's how resistance to change is a resource: it shows there is someone who still believes that saying how they look at the situation is worthwhile, somebody we can involve again if we listen to them. Take them seriously. Use their professionalism and involvement to take the things that make the change successful into account.

What is vitally important is therefore how the management chooses to deal with this kind of resistance, but also in the converse cases where new ideas or thoughts had been aired.

If an employee experiences that he or she is not listened to, then, as a rule, this person will seek recognition and sympathy elsewhere. He or she may complain during the lunch break, and this is naturally toxic to the organization.

Psychological security is therefore about ensuring that people feel comfortable with regard to sharing opinions and ideas but also that they feel that their opinions are heard, so it's not only when the criticism becomes shrill that it's heard.

As human beings, we can tolerate being told we're wrong, but we can't tolerate feeling that we're not being heard.

BECAUSE TRUE BELONGING ONLY HAPPENS WHEN WE PRESENT OUR AUTHENTIC, IMPERFECT SELVES TO THE WORLD, OUR SENSE OF BELONGING CAN NEVER BE GREATER THAN OUR LEVEL OF SELF-ACCEPTANCE.

Brené Brown

OTTO SCHARMER
The world of today and tomorrow

Otto Scharmer (Germany) is a senior lecturer at MIT, a Thousand Talents Program Professor at Tsinghua University, Beijing, and co-founder of the Presencing Institute (www.presencing.org). Scharmer chairs the MIT IDEAS program for cross-sector innovation, which helps leaders to innovative at the level of the whole system. He is the author of *Theory-U*, which has been translated into 20 languages, and co-author of Leading from the Emerging Future.

First and foremost, thank you for taking time to talk to *The GuruBook*. As editor of the book, I'm naturally grateful. I would like to start by looking at one of *The GuruBook's* main themes: *authentic leadership*. I have read that you believe leaders can train their ability to come closer to their authentic self. Can you explain that a little more closely?

I believe that we, as human beings, are not one person but two. We are the person, our present self, that we've become because of our journey through life—our past. In addition is our future self, which is the highest future potential that one can achieve as a human being.

The essence of authentic leadership, in my view, is to get these two parts of the self to listen to each other.

All of the great innovators and entrepreneurs that I've met are in a constant dialogue with the world and the universe. They are curious and seeking; that means they're listening to both their present and their future selves.

One good example of this is Route 128—a tech startup mecca. If you go down Route 128, you will of course meet a company striving after money; but money isn't the aim of these companies, it's just a result of what they do. The people on Route 128 are instead driven by something more profound. Their enthusiasm comes from a curiosity regarding the world and a desire to create another and better future. In many ways, they are authentic leaders.

Does this apply only to the Route 128 environment, or do you see it as a broader trend in the United States today?

It's quite clearly a broader trend. My experience tells me that what I said before doesn't just apply to tech entrepreneurs but many young people. I see it in part in the larger mainstream companies and partly in the next generation of leaders in the United States. I've met hundreds of promising leaders, some of them just a few years away from top jobs in the American business community. These people have chosen quite a conventional career, but most of them are not satisfied by their choice—they want more out of life.

That longing I've seen time and again. These young leaders have a deeper desire to recreate and rethink the world around them. They want to create a history they can be proud of.

I teach a subject at MIT that's called *U-Lab*. There, I meet a great many leaders from all over the world who are halfway through their careers, so to speak. When I ask them what they want out of life as a whole, and what has therefore brought them to MIT, I always get the same answer from them: "The higher up I get in my organization's internal hierarchy, the less inspired I feel by what my organization expects of me and wants me to do."

What they're saying, in other words, is that the higher they've climbed up the internal power ladder, the less meaningful they experience things and the further away they feel from the life they dream about. They experience a marked separation between their present and future selves—what they're doing today and who they might be tomorrow.

Why is this a problem?

Just take a look at the statistics. We're seeing in the United States an explosion in the number of depressions and leaders who burn out or, even worse, commit suicide.

When that's said, the statistics aren't just depressing reading. I also see countertrends and counterevidence in the form of young entrepreneurs who've got rich very quickly and who are now working on new and innovative ways of giving something back. Where the rich in the past typically gave something back in a very conventional way, these newly rich people are more innovative and entrepreneurial in their attempts to make the world a better place.

So if you see this as a strong trend, what does it mean for management tomorrow? In my view, the same books about leadership are written again and again. To be quite honest, there's not much that's new in them. Do the points you're making imply anything substantially new for management tomorrow?

In my view, they imply two vital new things.

The first has to do with what I call *broadening*. Our focus in management is often on the organizations, and I've said earlier that organizations today are either too big for the small problems or too small for the big problems. Let me explain that more closely.

The big problems could be climate change or the great inequality in the world. These problems are so massive that no organization will be in a position to solve them alone. This means that we have to establish new platforms for collaboration, which implies we must be able to coordinate very complex systems about human intentions.

What are human intentions? They are the common consciousness about society as a whole. When we think in that way, we experience a connection between all of the various sectors of society and all of the various types of companies and organizations. This is a new perspective that tomorrow's leaders must be aware of and take part in.

This also implies two other things, which I've chosen to call *turning inside out* and *turning outside in*.

We've seen this demonstrated, for instance, in the tech world, where companies have partly managed to turn inside out through crowdsourcing and co-creation methods with regard to developing new ideas, and partly been able to turn outside in when they invite people and partners from the world outside into their organizations.

We also see this in the health industry and in many other places, and the cleverest leaders manage to expand their consciousness from an ego focus to an ecosystem. They are aware of this gigantic network of relationships and potentials. In my view, what I've just said implies one new aspect of management.

I have chosen to call the other new aspect *deeping*, and that word is used to describe the spread of mindfulness and awareness in management.

The philosophy behind this new trend is that where you choose to focus is also where you put your energy. Mindfulness is today used in thousands of organizations, and the research in this area has exploded. Even the most traditional companies have started to use mindfulness in their leader training.

This way of coming into contact with your present self is probably more important than ever before for authentic leaders.

Lastly, can you suggest three things that the readers of *The GuruBook* should do after this interview. That is, if they've been inspired by your thoughts and opinions, how do they carry some of them out in their lives?

It's a matter of realizing, fundamentally, that Theory-U isn't a question of stabilizing the existing system, it's about disrupting it. The vision is to create a new world and develop new structures and ways of being, listening, and acting.

Therefore, I'd like to call on the readers to do three things:

1. If you haven't already done so, find a moment every day with mindfulness and peace. Listen to your present self. This may be a way for you to become aware that there are different levels of responsiveness.

2. Choose one or more people from your network, but no more than seven.

   Establish what I call a *deep listening circle* together with these people. The purpose of this circle is to support the participants' journeys as leaders, their change-maker journeys.

   It's important that the group isn't too big and that there are a large number of processes that can be used to create value and meaning in the group. You can get free inspiration from the U-Lab website (www.uschool.presencing.com).

The idea is that the group should meet quite often, and at every session the participants should give their full attention to one of the group's members and receive that person with an open heart and an open mind. You listen to them with the aim that they should develop as people and as leaders.

3. Be a part of U-Lab—a global ecosystem and group of change-makers from all sectors and types of organizations throughout the world. U-Lab is about refinding leadership and systems in politics, the business community, the financial sector, the health industry, and so on.

Participation in U-Lab is free, and in 2017, we're launching a global innovation ecosystem. The vision behind this is that many different systems should speak with each other and together make up a global movement for meaningful change.

TOM PETERS
Are you an 18-second manager?

Tom Peters (United States) is co-author of *In Search of Excellence*—the book that changed the way the world does business and which is often tagged as the best business book ever. Sixteen books and almost 30 years later, Peters is still at the forefront of the "management guru industry" he single-handedly invented.

A Harvard med school doc by the name of Jerome Groopman wrote a lovely book called *How Doctors Think*. And he begins by saying, "When you are engaging a patient, what is *the number one source* of evidence about that patient's problem?" And he answers with the obvious answer—duh!—"the patient." The patient won't use the right technical language, the signal-to-noise ratio won't be all that high. But in the course of a 5-, or 10-, or 15-minute discussion, you will pull out an incredible number of pearls.

Okay, the best source of information about a patient's ailment is the patient, *comma*. At that point, Groopman refers us or leads us to a research study that asks and then answers the following question

(but I'm going to halt for 3 seconds in here while you think of what your answer is): How long is it before the doctor addresses you, sits down with you; how long is it before the doctor, on average, interrupts?

And if you said, "18 seconds," you got it exactly right. Eighteen seconds and the doctor has interrupted with his opinion. Now, am I doing this little piece for you to trash doctors? Absolutely not. I'm doing this little piece to trash *you*, among the bosses who are watching this, and any of

us who are watching this who are experts or professionals or what have you. I bet you that among the bosses in the audience this that seven out of eight are 18-second bosses. That is, it is, "Oh my god, I've seen this before. This is what you should do," before you even express what the problem is.

So here's the segue. I have come to the conclusion, and you may argue that this is overstated, but I don't care whether you argue that or not; I believe it. The single most significant strategic strength that an organization can have is not a good strategic plan but a commitment to strategic listening on the part of every member of the organization: strategic listening to frontline employees, strategic listening to vendors, to customers.

Because you see, I really hate MBA programs, but some day I'm going to have my *own* MBA program. And the number-one core course in Tom's MBA program is going to be a two-part, half-year-each course called Strategic Listening I and Strategic Listening II. The reality is you can teach listening; you can get better at listening; there's no issue about that. But guess what? It's like playing the piano. It's like becoming an actor. It's like learning to be an artist. It is a profession that has to be learned. And it is my opinion that, as a leader or as a team member, that to a significant degree, your profession is listening. So think about it. Are you an 18-second manager? Bet you are.

Now Hear This! Listening Is the Ultimate "Core Competence."

Listening* is …

(*And when you read "listening," please substitute "*OBSESSION* with listening.")

Listening is … the ultimate mark of *Respect*.
Listening is … the heart and soul of *Engagement*.
Listening is … the heart and soul of *Kindness*.
Listening is … the heart and soul of *Thoughtfulness*.
Listening is … the basis for true *Collaboration*.
Listening is … the basis for true *Partnership*.
Listening is … a *Team Sport*.
Listening is … a *Developable Individual Skill*.*
(*Though women are *far* better at it than men.)
Listening is … the basis for *Community*.
Listening is … the bedrock of *Joint Ventures that work*.
Listening is … the bedrock of *Joint Ventures that last*.
Listening is … the core of *effective Cross-functional Communication**
(*Which is in turn Attribute #1 of organizational effectiveness.*)
Listening is … the engine of *superior EXECUTION*.
Listening is … the key to *making the Sale*.
Listening is … the key to *Keeping the Customer's Business*.
Listening is … the engine of *Network development*.
Listening is … the engine of *Network maintenance*.
Listening is … the engine of *Network expansion*.
Listening is … *Learning*.

Listening is … the *sine qua non of Renewal*.
Listening is … the *sine qua non of Creativity*.
Listening is … the *sine qua non of Innovation*.
Listening is … the core of *taking Diverse opinions aboard*.
Listening is … *Strategy*.
Listening is … *Source #1 of "Value-added."*
Listening is … *Differentiator #1*.
Listening is … *Profitable*.*
(*The "R.O.I." from listening is higher than that from any other single activity.)
Listening underpins … *Commitment to EXCELLENCE*.

Do you agree with the above?

If you agree, shouldn't listening be … *a Core Value?*
If you agree, shouldn't listening be … *perhaps Core Value #1?**
(*"We are Effective Listeners—we treat Listening EXCELLENCE as the Centerpiece of our Commitment to Respect and Engagement and Community and Growth"—or some such.)
If you agree, shouldn't listening be … *a Core Competence?*
If you agree, shouldn't listening be … *Core Competence #1?*
If you agree, shouldn't listening be … *an explicit "agenda item" at every meeting?*
If you agree, shouldn't listening be … *our Strategy—per se? (Listening = Strategy.)*
If you agree, shouldn't listening be … *the #1 skill we look for in Hiring (for every job)?*
If you agree, shouldn't listening be … *the #1 attribute we examine in our Evaluations?*
If you agree, shouldn't listening be … *the #1 skill we look for in Promotion decisions?*
If you agree, shouldn't listening be … *the #1 Training priority at every stage of everyone's career—from Day #1 to Day LAST?*

If you agree, what are you going to do about it … *in the next 30 MINUTES?*

If you agree, what are you going to do about it … *at your NEXT meeting?*

If you agree, what are you going to do about it … *by the end of the DAY?*

If you agree, what are you going to do about it … *in the next 30 DAYS?*

If you agree, what are you going to do about it … *in the next 12 MONTHS?*

Used by permission of Tom Peters. See tompeters.com for more information.

INDEX

H

I

J

K

L

m